Dedication

To all the mental health professionals, physicians, brain researchers, educators, life-coaches, family members, and organizations throughout the world who work, unceasingly, to improve the quality of life for autistic children and adults

Other Books by Jennie Spallone

Fiction

Psychobabble

Fatal Reaction

Window of Guilt

Deadly Choices

Smashing Castles

How a Young Autistic Woman Discovered Her Authentic Self

Jennie Spallone, M.A.

Contents

Acknowledgments

I WOULD LIKE TO thank my husband, Rocco, for patiently holding down the fort while I followed where God led.

Thank you, God, for working through me to better this young woman's life and allowing me to build a safe environment where all my students and clients can develop their self-esteem. At the gut level, they need to recognize that they are deserving of love and respect and must refuse to accept anything less.

I would especially like to thank Akira for allowing me to share her story with the world. We are richer for it.

Preface

Akira Stone, a young woman whose psychological diagnosis reads autism, once told me that "People with autism just need one person to believe in them." I was fortunate to life coach Akira for eighteen months. I did believe in her, and I helped her along the difficult path toward believing in herself. As parents, teachers, tutors, therapists, child advocates, and all who care about improving the lives of children with special needs, it is important to focus on what makes our clients function from the inside out, not just from what meets the eye.

The autism spectrum ranges from non-verbal, low-functioning individuals who require constant care throughout their lives to the child protégé whose genius is apparent, but whose social skills lag far behind. Akira's skill level puts her smack dab in the middle of these two extremes. Her childhood Asperger's label has been phased out under the general term, autism spectrum. Yet, Akira is highly verbal, focused in her writing, and becoming more and more socially adept every day.

When I taught high school at a private K-12 school for students with special needs, I had a high-functioning autistic student in my journalism class. He'd undergone years of speech therapy, social skills training, and scored well academically, but when it came to carrying on a conversation, he only responded in monosyllables.

One month into taking my journalism class, this young man was successfully following a three-question script as he interviewed teachers for our school newspaper. While no golden-tongued god, he was able to confront his fear of verbally interacting with an authority figure.

When I first arrived on Akira's doorstep, I encountered a young adult who suffered from a different kind of fear, the constant fear of being told by her sister that she was inept and useless. I soon discovered the negative impact this disrespect had on Akira's self-esteem.

But this story boasts a happy ending. It shows, as Akira says, that people with autism—but really all of us—just need one person to believe in them. One person to shine the light on what *might be*. One person to guide us toward our destiny.

Despite well-intentioned professional support, a child's parent or guardian possesses the ultimate power to either fling open the shutters to a shining future or destroy new possibilities. The words we use, the facial expressions we project, the actions we employ, communicate respect or disdain for an individual.

Akira's truth is our gift to you. God bless you and those you are caring for. You make all the difference.

Sincerely,

Jennie Spallone, M.A.

Learning Disabilities Specialist/ADD & Autism Life Coach

First Meeting

Legal pad in hand, I bang the brass knocker. Given my knowledge of autism, plus Mark Stone's caveat about his daughter's maturity level, I expect to meet a young woman who is low-functioning autistic. A twenty-six-year-old would be well past the age of flapping her wings as she runs through the house. Yet I picture her talking in monosyllables. No eye contact. Staring into space.

If Akira is higher up on the autism spectrum, I prepare to endure a monologue on the natural habitat of the Venus flytrap or a discourse on the preponderance of dust bunnies due to climate change. Of course, Mark could be exaggerating about his daughter's deficits.

A tall, lanky man with a receding hairline introduces himself as Mark. He ushers me into a spacious family room with a high ceiling and gestures to a chocolate-colored La-Z-Boy chair, flanked by an unlit red brick fireplace.

Mark crosses the room to join a pale-faced young woman sitting on a brown leather sofa, a small dog in her lap. "Akira, this is Jennie, your new life coach."

A flicker of surprise sweeps her eyes. Then her expression goes blank. "Hello," she whispers.

Evidently Dad has kept secret from his daughter our meeting's objective, or perhaps even the meeting itself.

"Thanks for inviting me into your home. How can I help?"

Mark begins. "My wife died ten months ago, after five years of struggling with ovarian cancer. It's really taken a toll on our family. We are still suffering."

"I'm so sorry for your loss," I mumble. What else can one say in such a sad situation?

"My wife was the one who took Akira to college classes all these years. She made sure my daughter received the special services she required. Now that my wife is gone, I doubt whether I can fill her shoes. Annie, Akira's younger sister, already lives on her own, while Akira has never been to a grocery store or a shopping mall by herself."

I notice Akira flinch at his words.

"What concerns me most," continues Mark, "is whether Akira will be able to live independently after I die."

"Independent living is a concern many parents of adult children with disabilities share," I say. "There are group homes for young adults with autism."

"My wife and I checked into that possibility before she died. There's a waiting list of several years. Akira may not even qualify."

I turn to the young woman. She's nibbling on her nails. "What are your thoughts about someday living on your own?"

"I want to learn how to take care of myself, but I'm not sure whether I can live away from Dad."

Responds in complete sentences, I scribble on my pad.

"How is she going to live on her own when she has no driver's license and no job?" Mark muses.

"You never made a big deal about it before now," Akira says timidly. "You said you liked having me live with you because it gives you something to focus on besides needing to mow our large yard."

Mark doesn't respond.

"Did you attend college?" I ask Akira.

"She actually received an associate's degree in general education." Mark grimaces. "Took her eight years to get it."

Akira scratches the crown of her head.

"Lots of people work and go to school at the same time," I say.

The young woman shakes her head. "I changed majors three times. Then my mom got sick and I had to drive her to chemo twice a week."

No fixation on single topic. A good sign.

"How long ago did you receive your degree?"

Dad rushes in. "She's been out of school for three years."

"Have you ever held a job?"

"I did stock work at a department store and at a pet shop."

"She was fired from the department store and left the pet shop to help care for my wife," Mark says.

I'm no social worker, but I sense a palpable resentment behind the father's words.

Nothing unusual, there. When given an opportunity to vent, parents of children with disabilities often lash out at the injustice of it all.

Akira glances down at her lap.

"What caused you to get fired?" I ask.

"She'd oversleep," says Mark. "She spends fourteen to sixteen hours a day upstairs in her room playing video games. Often, she'll role play for fourteen hours straight, not even stopping to eat or drink."

Dad just can't restrain himself from replying in his daughter's stead. I turn to the young woman. "Did you ask your manager to schedule you for a later shift?"

Akira and her dad shake their heads in unison.

Advocacy training needed, I note. "How much were you making per hour at the department store?"

Once again, it is Mark's voice I hear. "Minimum wage."

I attempt to engage Akira in conversation. "If you could do any kind of work, what would it be?"

Now Akira's eyes glow with excitement. "I'd love to design video games."

"Gaming was her third major," scoffs Mark. "It was a disaster."

Akira nods miserably. "The semester final was nerve-wracking. We had to write strings of code. I walked out and didn't finish the test."

Test anxiety, I write.

"You're three years older and wiser, now. Would you consider going back and trying again?"

"She's already attempted computer programming, graphic arts, and gaming. I'm not wasting any more money on her education." Dad is extremely frustrated. "She's got to get a job."

"The thing is, Mark, seven dollars and fifty cents per hour isn't going to cut it if you want Akira to eventually live on her own. She needs to train in a technical program that will guarantee her a living wage."

"She needs a job, not more training," Dad retorts.

Akira clasps her hands tightly. "I'm not sure if I'm ready to go back to school."

I switch gears. "Have you ever been tested for learning disabilities or ADD?"

Akira shakes her head.

"She had years of pragmatics training back east."

Pragmatics training is social skills training taught by social workers or psychologists. It has zilch to do with academics and everything to do with role-playing social situations, like "How can you tell if somebody is being sarcastic?" or "How do I ask if there's space for me to sit at the school lunch table?"

"Were you better in language arts or in math?"

"She wrote a couple of decent essays when she was in high school," says Mark.

"How about we begin by doing a reading and written expression assessment to discover her strengths and weaknesses? The tests will give us a baseline. Then we can move on from there."

Mark and his daughter hesitantly agree.

"We'll begin tomorrow. Before I go, I'd like to do a quick student interview to get to know you, if that's okay?"

Akira's eyes widen.

"It's just a questionnaire about your likes and dislikes."

She smiles wanly.

"Favorite color?"

"I like pretty much any shade of blue," she responds.

"Favorite movie?"

"*Rush Hour*. No matter how many times I watch it, I can never stop laughing."

"Favorite book?"

"I love the *Dragon Riders of Pern* series and a lot of fantasy type books. I haven't read any in a while, though."

"Hobbies?"

"I like to draw anime, play video games with my friends, and watch Japanese cartoons."

"Do you ever journal?"

"Not so often," she says.

Her shrug tells me never.

"Tell me three words people use to describe you."

Akira appears stymied.

I rephrase the question. "How would your friends describe you?"

"Uh . . . loyal, carefree, friendly?"

Seeks approval, I note.

"Tell me something that makes you special."

There is a long pause as Akira considers the question. "I'm not judgmental, and it takes a lot to make me angry."

Such introspection in a young person with Asperger's is unusual. I turn to Mark. "When was the last time you had your daughter retested for autism?"

"Not since her pediatrician first diagnosed her at age 10."

"As a former special education teacher, I don't see defining signs that appear on the autism spectrum. I can give you a referral to get her retested by a psychologist."

Mark waves off my suggestion. "For now, let's just have Akira do your testing and move on from there."

"Sounds good." I gather up my evaluation materials and head for the door.

My initial conversation with Mark led me to assume that his twenty-six-year-old daughter was functioning at the level of a high school student. Although far from a happy camper, Akira's intelligence and introspective ability definitely negates that assumption. *Is she really autistic?* I wonder. Depression, anxiety, or self-esteem issues might be the real culprit. My curiosity is peaked.

"See you tomorrow." I bid Akira and her father adieu, hoping tomorrow's diagnostics will provide clarity.

As soon as I pull into my garage, I phone Geri, my special education teacher friend back in Chicago. She's been teaching autistic students for decades. If anyone can explain what's going on, it's her. I shut off the ignition, then blurt out, "I think my new client was misdiagnosed."

"And a good day to you, too," Geri says heartily.

"Sorry. Didn't mean to bowl you over," I say. Then I tell her the whole story.

"You've taught autistic high school kids," she replies. "You know what signs to look for."

"Yeah, but the two autistic high school students I taught at COVE were bright but lacked Akira's communication skills." I neglect to mention I'd stretched the truth with Akira and her dad, regarding the extent of my autism expertise.

"First of all, there's a complete range of abilities, even on the high end of the spectrum," says Geri.

"You're talking musical protégé or math genius," I say, "or the successful nerds who enter the work force in computer programming, technology, and game design. But how many of these people excel in expressive and written language?"

"Look, you've only met this gal one time. Do your testing. Start working with her. Then see if you still feel the same way. Just remember, you're a special education teacher, not a psychologist. You can't diagnose who does and doesn't have autism."

"I know, I know."

Just then, my hubby walks in the door from volunteering at the local food pantry. "Talk to you soon," I tell Geri.

As I click off the phone, I debate whether my gut feeling can be trusted.

Test Day

THE NEXT AFTERNOON, I arrive at the Stone house, test booklets in hand. The GSRT (Gray Silent Reading Test) and the GORT-3 (Gray Oral Reading Test) test students through age twenty-one, while the norms for the TOAL-3—Test of Adolescent and Adult Language—tests students through age twenty-five.

Although Akira is twenty-six, these tests will provide a reliable indicator of Akira's abilities in reading fluency, reading comprehension, phonemic awareness, spelling, vocabulary, and written expression. I usually tutor young kids, so I'm not keen to purchase an expensive set of test materials for one older student.

Akira greets me at the door with greasy-looking hair and a half-hearted "Hello." She tentatively ushers me into the kitchen. I hesitate to set my testing materials on a placemat dotted with toast crumbs. She appears oblivious of my dilemma. "Think you can remove this placemat and wipe the table?"

"Sure." She grabs a brand-new looking sponge from the kitchen sink.

"Could I also trouble you for a glass of water?"

Akira runs to the guest bathroom. Then she returns with a paper mouthwash cup filled with water. Hmm. People with autism usually take words literally.

Akira finally joins me at the kitchen table. I hand her a written expression test booklet. Her face pales. "I haven't studied for this.

I've never been very good at taking tests. I'd go to class having studied what I thought was a decent amount and then go completely blank come test time."

My voice automatically slips into its warmest, most consoling tone. "This is not a high-stakes test like you had in school. Your father, you, and I are the only ones who will see the results, unless you work with a psychologist again someday."

Dad has confided that Akira saw a psychologist during her mother's illness. Those visits ceased upon Mom's death.

Akira scratches the crown of her head.

"Seriously, we're simply going to find out what English language skills you possess."

"Okay," she whispers.

Special education professionals debate whether autism is the new ADD (attention deficit disorder), a label that everybody and his brother seem to be getting during recent times. They ponder whether a non-verbal learning disability is a more accurate assessment.

In non-verbal learning disabilities, a glaring discrepancy exists between a child's non-verbal versus expressive language. Many of these students excel in math over language arts.

But unlike students with non-verbal learning deficits, kids with high-functioning autism often repeat, ad nauseam, data on one topic—the topic of that individual child's focus—usually some obscure fact no one else gives a hoot about.

I flip to the TOAL-3: Listening/Vocabulary. "In this thirty-five-item picture-vocabulary subtest, place an 'x' on two pictures that relate to the word I tell you.

"Plane."

Akira puts an "X" on the airplane and also on the carpenter using a plane to smooth new flooring.

We move on to the Listening/Grammar Subtest, where Akira needs to choose two sentences read to her which have the same meaning. She grins. "This is like playing Two Truths and a Lie."

Never heard of that game, but whatever. Now, I administer the Speaking/Vocabulary Subtest, which requires Akira to produce a meaningful sentence using the correct meaning of each stimulus word I read. She sails through the subtest.

Next, we move on to the thirty-item Speaking/Grammar Subtest, in which I ask Akira to repeat each sentence I read to her. Once she completes this test, we move onto the Reading/Vocabulary Subtest. Akira is yawning—heck, so am I.

Akira senses something's not right. She begins to apologize. "It probably looks like I'm not paying attention. I didn't sleep well last night. I was afraid I'd oversleep and miss your arrival."

"We're almost done," I assure her. "If we break now, it's definitely nap time for both of us." I flip the cardboard test book to the Writing/Vocabulary subtest, which sparks Akira's attention. She reads a stimulus word, and then writes a meaningful sentence using that word in the exact form given. No homonyms.

The sun is shifting in the sky as we finally alight on the Writing/ Grammar Subtest. Akira must combine each set of three sentences into one sentence, using grammatically complex construction.

Finished! I gather my materials and head toward the door. "Great job. I'll come back tomorrow to test your reading."

"Uh huh. Bye."

Akira closes the door behind me. Exhausted, I shuffle down the stairs leading to my car. It has been a successful testing experience. Akira readily engaged with both the test questions and me.

Next morning, I wait patiently for Akira to once again remove the offensive placemats and wipe down the kitchen table. Old habits die hard.

I luck out. Today, Akira hands me a glass—rather than a paper cup—of water.

We take our seats. Akira's cheeks have more color today.

I lay a test booklet before her. "Today you are going to take the GORT-3 oral and silent reading tests."

The GORT-3 tests students through eighteen years, eleven months. Yes, my client is twenty-six, but at least this will give me some informal results. It examines a student's oral reading fluency and listening comprehension for paragraphs and multi-choice questions, and also performs a miscue (mistakes) analysis to determine wherein the problem lies.

We begin with a 130-word baseball game story passage normally administered to students at the twelfth-grade level.

Akira scratches her head. "I don't watch baseball."

"No problem. Just read the paragraph aloud, and then answer the questions."

The five questions include literal, inference, critical thinking, abstract reasoning, and prediction. Akira fluently reads each passage and answers the comprehension questions.

Thirty minutes later, she's completed the whole darn book. "Great job, kiddo."

"Whew. I didn't think I did that well."

I give Akira a quick smile and substitute the GSRT—Gray Silent Reading Test—appropriate for students through age twenty-five. This silent-reading test poses literal, inferential, and critical thinking questions. It also elicits personal/emotional responses to an increasingly difficult series of silently read passages.

Akira zooms through the silent reading test, just as she did on the previous tests.

"I've got a feeling these tests will indicate that you function at a much higher level than both you and your dad expect."

"If that happens, my sister will be really shocked, too."

I glance up at her. "Why do you say that?"

Akira picks at the skin on her fingernails. "Annie always tells me how stupid I am. She always picks fights, which makes me always have to defend myself."

Curiosity gets the best of me. "Fist fights?"

My client shakes her head. "More like screaming fights."

"Like when?"

She grimaces. "She'll scream from downstairs that I spend an obscene amount of hours playing stupid online games with people I don't even know, although they claim to be my friends. 'Dad's going to be stuck with you living at home forever,'" she mimics her sister.

"Those words must really hurt," I empathize.

"Heck, yeah."

"How do you respond?"

"I tell her just because these people are on the internet doesn't make them any less my real friends. Unlike her, they treat me with respect. But Annie shouts back that unless I've met these people face to face, they don't count as friends.

"From our upstairs landing, I see her storm into the living room to pull the internet plug. I rush down the stairs to stop her, trip on the two bottom stairs, and smash into the back door. Annie pays no attention to my moment of pain. She's too intent on pulling the plug."

My jaw drops; an autistic client is actually relating a complete story to me!

"Then Dad bursts into the living room from his home office. 'What the hell is going on here? I was in the middle of an International Internet conference. Whichever one of you disconnected the internet, plug it back in now!'"

I'm hooked into Akira's story. "How did it turn out?"

Akira hangs her head. "This war between Annie and me never ends. There's rarely a moment of peace in our house when she comes to visit. It was even worse before she moved out."

"Oh?" I ask.

"One day, Annie barged into my bedroom. I was kneeling on the carpet, talking to my boyfriend on my laptop. She demanded I get off my stupid computer and go with her to get ice cream instead of spending time with my 'fake boyfriend.' In the beginning, she didn't think he was real. It wasn't until he came from the Netherlands to visit and brought me a soccer cup full of Dutch chocolate that she changed her tune.

"I told her I wasn't in the mood for ice cream, but she told me we were going anyway. Why couldn't she take a hint that I'd rather spend time with a stranger who understood me rather than a blood relative who treated me like shit?"

"How did you react?"

"I stuck my fingers in my ears and sang, 'La, la, la, I can't hear you.' With no warning, Annie stomped my laptop closed. The entire operating system crashed. I panicked. 'You broke my laptop. Are you out of your fucking mind? Get the fuck out of my room or I'm calling Dad.'

"She snorted and told me I'm pathetic and to 'watch my language' She didn't even care if she'd broken my laptop. Then she casually walked out of my room, acting like nothing was wrong, leaving me to tend to my broken computer."

"How old was she at the time?"

"Nineteen and I was twenty-one. But nothing's changed. I'm twenty-six years old now, and my sister still knows how to destroy my self-esteem. She tries to convince me I'm retarded. She brainwashes me into thinking I am useless and worthless. She claims my friends only interact with me out of pity."

Nobody deserves this foul treatment. "Do you buy into her portrayal of you?"

Akira shrugs. "Every time she insults me, I feel more like a puppet than a human being. I always wonder why Dad doesn't tell her to stop. It feels like he just wants us to duke it out until one of us gives up or ends up dead."

This is serious stuff she's talking about. "Did your family go to counseling when you guys were growing up?'

"Only twice. The second time, Annie told the psychologist 'This is bullshit' and ran out of the room."

"Was Annie's behavior different when your mom was alive?"

"A bit. Mom would sit my sister down and tell her that she was causing more harm than good. Unfortunately, Mom is gone, and I'm left to fend for myself."

"I am so sorry you've had to endure such disrespectful treatment. We really need to find you a psychologist."

Akira waves me off. "Dad won't spend any more money on counseling."

I sigh. "How can I help?"

Akira pauses to consider my question. Then she says, "I just need someone who can prove to me that the real me is just as amazing as my video-game avatar. I highly doubt that person exists."

I pat her shoulder and say, "Never say never."

As I walk out the door, I wonder if maybe that person is me.

Moving Forward

THE STONE FAMILY AND I sit across from their unlit fireplace. I give Mark a copy of my written report. Akira's hands are trembling, so I present a user-friendly, oral summary. "Bottom line, Akira is functioning above average in both oral and silent reading comprehension."

Akira's hands begin to steady.

"Your daughter scored above average in reading and written vocabulary, and average in speaking vocabulary, as well as oral and written grammar. Listening/Grammar is the only subtest in which she scored below average. Overall, Akira scored at the eighty-seventh percentile."

Akira's voice is incredulous. "Really? I always thought my vocabulary and grammar were bad."

Dad appears surprised, as well.

I turn to Mark. "Do you want me to test Akira in math or should we move on to developing a life skills program?"

"Let's move forward in developing a plan," he says.

Thank goodness. Before morphing into my new career as a life coach, I'd donated my math and general curriculum tests to another of my special education teacher friends.

I pull my legal pad from my canvas bag. "You both assigned

independence as a long-term goal for Akira. What does that word symbolize to each of you?"

I glance at Akira. Would she grasp the relationship between *word* and *symbolize*?

Absence of perplexed expression, I note. Still, she does remain silent, allowing her dad to fill the void. "I want her to be able to maintain a physical hygiene routine."

"Are we talking shampoo and shower?"

Mark nods. "Right now, she only showers once a week. That's just not acceptable."

Akira stiffens.

I jot down the request. "What else?"

"She needs to change the kitty litter once a day and set up a schedule to feed the dog."

"You feed her in the morning, Dad," Akira protests.

"The dog needs to eat twice a day now, because of her health problems."

"Noted. What else?"

Mark rushes in with his next request. "She needs to learn to cook and cook at least twice a week."

I turn to Akira. "Learning to cook can relieve some of your dad's burden when he comes home tired from work."

Akira nods. "Before she passed away, Mom put together a binder of recipes she cut out from magazines. She gave one to me and one to my sister."

"So that could be a warm, fuzzy way of feeling your mom's presence."

Akira smiles at me. "I guess."

I bullet all three suggestions. "What else?"

Mark doesn't hesitate. It's like he's been waiting to unload for two decades. "She needs to pass her driving test, and she needs to get a job."

I gasp. A twenty-six-year-old woman not having a driver's license? The family resides in a country setting, a good fifteen minutes from the nearest grocery store—or any store, for that matter. "Have you ever had a driver's license?"

Akira shakes her head. "Just a learning permit. Still, I drove my mom to her cancer treatments."

"How far away was that?"

"Hour-and-a-half round trip."

This girl is just one revelation after another. "And after your mom died?"

Mark continues. "Even earlier on, my wife and I didn't feel Akira could be trusted to drive alone."

I glance at Akira. "Did you ever want to drive on your own?"

Her hands tremble. "Yes."

"So, except for your mom or dad driving you somewhere, you've stayed in the house for the last three years?"

Akira nods.

A stringy-haired Rapunzel locked in her tower. No wonder she stays up until all hours playing video games. "How about buying an electric scooter, just to get you to the grocery store?"

"We don't have any sidewalks around here. Cars go well past the speed limit. It would be way too dangerous for Akira."

"Besides," says Akira, "Dad does all the shopping."

I sit up straight. "This time, you will take your driver's test and pass."

Both Akira and her father look at me dubiously, but I pay them no heed. Motivation and persistence positively impact outcome. "You mentioned jobs."

"The problem is, I'd have to drive her back and forth from work," says Mark. "With my busy schedule, that won't work."

I hesitate, but only for a millisecond. Problem solving is my forte. "Akira, you said you love dogs and cats, right?"

"Uh huh."

"How about starting a pet sitting business?"

"But how would I get around?"

Good question. The houses on her block each sit on an acre of land. It would take lots of legwork to put flyers in each door. "Do you do yoga, exercise, dance, or walk the dog?"

Akira shakes her head. "The dog pees in the backyard. We have an elliptical machine upstairs, but I never use it."

"An exercise regimen is important for your health. Distributing fifty flyers over a two-week period will strengthen your cardiovascular system. It's doable."

Akira smiles. "My mom was a nutritionist. Always trying to get me to walk."

I add walking and pet sitting service to our list of goals. "Anything else?"

Akira and her father shake their heads.

"Attending temple services and volunteering in the community are two goals I would like to add."

"If she wants to go," says Mark, half-heartedly.

"I'm not sure," says Akira.

"No worries. It's something we can revisit." I read the list aloud to them. "Which three goals do you want to start with?"

"I'd say personal grooming is the most important thing," says Mark. "Cleaning the cat litter box, feeding the dog, and doing a couple of daily chores around the house should come next. Cooking dinner twice a week would be third; I don't care if it's tacos or spaghetti, just something edible."

"What are your thoughts, Akira?"

"That all sounds good."

"All right. Next week we start on grooming."

"Eventually, Akira needs to be put on some kind of schedule so she's not on the computer all day and night," says Mark.

I pop my legal pad back into my canvas bag. "Will do."

As I head out the door, I assure both Akira and her father these goals are attainable. It just takes time, effort, and persistence.

They don't know it yet, but they're working with the Energizer Bunny.

Family Life

As a special education teacher for grades 1 through 12, I *was* the Energizer Bunny. What an adrenaline rush it was to plan and present yet another lesson using multisensory learning techniques.

However, as a teacher, I would obsess about the one student sitting in the back row who cradled his head in his arms during my entire lesson. Why hadn't I been able to reach him?

Each year, I'd park myself in front of yet another school principal, asking what resources were available for a particular student. Other times, I'd request permission for our special education kids to volunteer at the local preschool.

I attributed my annoying habits of blurting out and interrupting others to the attention-seeking behavior of a child growing up in a divorced family. Without child support, my mother worked six days a week just to put food on the table. She only *heard* me when I asked her to help plan a creative project, solve a personal or academic problem, or take me and a friend somewhere fun.

I didn't realize I was ADHD myself until I taught an ADD course to general education teachers seeking continuing education credits. Attention deficit disorder regulates reasoning, planning, and impulsivity.

My ADHD (now called ADD) turned out to be a blessing. It enabled me to teach my students and my own children to live fearlessly, to explore a life filled with possibilities.

My mother was the original Energizer Bunny. She applauded my talents, encouraged me to work hard, be resourceful, and never give up.

It is amazing how we either duplicate or skirt the life lessons we learned from our parents and teachers. Although we may resolve to be different, those life lessons are poised over the default button, tempting us to raise our children the same way we were raised.

I wonder what life lessons Akira learned from her mother and father. Did she receive the "We celebrate your uniqueness" message or the message that said, "Don't make a fool of yourself in public?"

Who am I to judge? I have not raised a child who is on the autism spectrum. I can only imagine the emotional and physical toll such a diagnosis takes on parents. The frustration and fatigue parents experience after years of battling the school system and social service agencies. The desperation parents feel over obsessing over how their adult child will survive after they are gone.

But what I can't fathom is how a parent can stand by and allow another family member to verbally, physically, or sexually abuse their child without intervening. A child with special needs deserves to be respected, not just from others but from herself/himself. Teaching our children that their thoughts and emotions deserve respect, even when they're pre-school age, is the first step to developing healthy self-esteem.

I once tutored a young student whose father bragged to my face about whipping her when she was *bad*. I suggested he watch Super Nanny on TV to learn other discipline techniques. He boasted that his daughter would never be *whupped* by a husband any worse than the *whupping* she got from him. I reported the father to the rural police officer because I feared what he'd do to his new baby, due within days. Muttering that this guy had no history of arrest, the police officer grudgingly agreed to go check out their trailer and talk to the father. I cringe to think about the verbal and physical abusive messages this little girl will grow up experiencing. And on and on, generation after generation, unless someone or something intervenes to break the cycle.

I don't know much about Akira Stone's family yet. I truly hope her childhood was filled with a collage of positive messages, such as "Way to go!" "You're doing great!" "You will succeed!"

No matter the color of Akira's life messages, I pray, as her life coach, to shoot an iridescent marble into her bowl of self-esteem.

Self-grooming

Today, I introduce Akira to a daily schedule that includes self-grooming, chores, nutrition, sleep, exercise, and job search. As a former high school special education teacher, I wrote and taught from a written expression book that included these life skills, along with numerous others.

The irony is that strict adherence to a time schedule makes my brain itch. My weekdays/nights are set in brick with scheduled tutoring sessions and extracurricular events. But my weekends are free-flow.

However, Akira's daily schedule is blank, unless you count the fourteen to sixteen hours per day she spends playing video games. It doesn't help that she sleeps until noon because she doesn't go to sleep until two a.m.

We fill in the blanks on the green weekly calendar:

- MWF shower/wash, condition, and blow-dry hair.

- MWF ten to twenty minutes on elliptical.

- M–F 2:00 p.m. to 4:00 p.m.: Job search/email resumes

- M–F 5:00 p.m.: Feed dog.

- T & TH 5:30 p.m.: Cook dinner. (Dad cooks dinner the rest of the week.)

When I tell Akira she needs to shut down her computer at eleven p.m. on weeknights and set her alarm for nine a.m. every weekday morning, she is aghast. Her dad sees my proposed schedule and shares his own doubts. "I understand her resistance to the new time schedule. It's not as if she's working."

Hello. He was the one who had rated her sleep schedule as high priority. "This sleep schedule will strengthen her resolve so when she does get a job, she'll already be in the habit of getting up at a reasonable time," I say.

"She'll never keep to that schedule," predicts Mark.

Nice to know we're all on the same page, I think.

I move on to basic grooming. "You need to shower and wash your hair three times a week," I say. Heck, I don't even wash my own hair three times a week, but I figure she might at least get two weekly shampoos in.

When Mark excuses himself to go to the bathroom, I draw my chair nearer to Akira. "You will eventually need to shop for your own personal hygiene items. No more relying on your dad for things like that."

Akira's eyes begin to tear.

"What's wrong?"

"I don't know if I can live up to all of Dad's expectations, detailed as they are."

"No worries. We're starting with goals only slightly above your comfort level."

"Way above my comfort level," says Akira.

"Listen, you've got what it takes to reach these goals. It's just going to take time and patience."

"I can't even remember if I fed the dog today. How in the world am I supposed to remember a week's worth of showering, shampooing, and feeding the puppy?"

I refuse to toss solutions at Akira like darts at a dartboard. Authentic learning involves brainstorming solutions. "What memory technique would work for you in this situation?"

Akira pauses. "Would setting timers on my phone be helpful? My phone is on the other side of my bedroom. I could set one alarm to feed Misty and another alarm to take her out. I'll have to get up from the bed or the computer to go turn it off.

"When I spend all my time on the computer, I lose track of time. On top of that, I tune out everything around me, so I'll probably end up missing some of my alarms."

"Trust me, Akira, you've got this."

Shopping Spree

TODAY, OUR FIRST STOP is Ulta Cosmetics. Akira and I are shopping for self-care items. Most young women in their twenties view acne and dandruff as scourges to eliminate. But beauty concerns have zipped past Akira's radar like a bullet on steroids. "I don't think I even have a valid makeup kit," she remarks in an embarrassed tone.

Not so strange. How much makeup does a person really need when she spends her whole life glued to a video game monitor?

Akira pretends not to care. "Honestly, I never wear much makeup to begin with."

A customer associate helps Akira find hypoallergenic makeup that matches her pale skin tone; concealer, blush, and lip-gloss are the only makeup Akira needs.

Akira's current shampoo is a generic anti-dandruff one from the local drugstore, and she isn't worried about her acne. Unbelievable for a young woman in 2018! After perusing the shelves, we settle on a hydrating shampoo and conditioner, along with body wash.

Next, we wander down the hypoallergenic facial scrub aisle, taking a detour through the biting fingernails section. Akira chooses a concoction that promises to put the kibosh on her habit. *Are Akira's nail biting and acne caused by anxiety or poor nutrition?* I wonder.

Akira's says her sister shops at Ulta, so she decides to open her own account at the checkout counter.

Minutes later, we head out to the parking lot. "So how did you feel about the shopping experience?" I ask.

Akira grins. "Proud of myself. The whole experience was a confidence booster."

Once back in the car, I ask Akira why she doesn't shop with her sister.

"Both Dad and Annie treat me like I'm mentally challenged. We always argue. Every time I do something well, my sister squashes it."

How ironic. Akira's sister attends graduate school, majoring in child development; her master's thesis is on father attachment. My client is living like a visitor in her own home.

As we pull up to Ross Department Store, Akira confides the only jewelry she owns is heirlooms from her mother and grandmother, plus a few necklaces from an aunt. No fun costume jewelry. No colorful necklaces or charm bracelets.

Granted, not all girls love Claire's or Charming Charlie's, although my own daughters used to enjoy shopping there. Akira's retreat from all that glitters might simply indicate disinterest. Then again, that disinterest might signify she doesn't feel deserving of simple pleasures and frivolities.

"Since Mom died, no one has taken me shopping for clothes or jewelry," she says. Akira lacks positive female role models, and her mother's relatives live out-of-state. Without access to a car, Akira must depend on her dad to take her places.

Earlier this afternoon, Akira showed me her bedroom closet. Her total wardrobe consists of a handful of clothing appropriate for a weekend getaway. My kids each own at least triple that amount.

When I ask about her scarcity of clothes, Akira shrugs. "Since

I don't really consider myself that pretty, I basically don't dress up. My wardrobe is just T-shirts, polos, and khakis or jeans. I barely ever touch my few dressy dresses."

We're just about to step inside Ross when Akira freezes. "I'm really not a big fan of shopping. I go through sensory overload in department stores—the lights, the sounds, the crowds."

"I'll be right by your side," I reassure her. "If you feel squeamish, we'll leave."

Akira takes a deep breath. Then she follows me into the store. She plans to buy two dresses for the Jewish High Holidays and a nice outfit to wear if she goes out with friends. She stops again. "This store is gigantic. I'm not going to find anything for my tiny figure."

Akira is unaware of her actual body image, I think. Tiny is size 1 to 5. Although slim, she's probably a size 10, and she stands 5 feet 4 inches. "We won't know until we try," I say, taking her arm.

Together, we dig through the dress rack for something to fit her skinny frame. I choose a couple of dresses for her to try on. Already, I envision myself assuaging her anxiety as she attempts to make her choices.

My choices look way too matronly on Akira. She searches the racks on her own, expertly ferrets out three dresses, and heads for the dressing room. I wait outside the door to give my opinion.

The first dress is a turquoise color V-neck, perfect for late spring/early summer. "How about this one?" She performs a slow pirouette.

I give her a thumbs up.

Akira gives me a sheepish grin and disappears back into the dressing room to try on a royal blue dress. "This dress is a bit tighter than the previous one, but it makes me look like an actual adult, which is surprising since people always mistake me for being eighteen," she says.

My assumptions are set ablaze. "For someone who claims she doesn't like clothes you have good taste."

In the end, Akira chooses one turquoise dress and one purple dress. "I'm getting these," she says. No wringing of hands over her decision. Me? I ask at least three other women in the dressing room how I look before I decide on a dress.

Flushed with success, Akira loads a couple of shirts and pants, along with a pair of sparkly sandals and a pair of dress shoes, into her shopping cart, along with the two dresses.

Earlier, I asked the cashier if there were any job openings. Now Akira is at the cash register, following up without my reminder. Soon she and the cashier are chatting about the weather. Akira grins and says, "Wait five minutes and the temperature will drop thirty degrees."

Mark has repeatedly referred to Akira's poor social skills. But I see that Akira is far from damaged goods. All she needs is an opportunity to shine.

Kitchen Duty

Akira and I skim through the recipe book her mom bequeathed her. For our first cooking session, we look for a simple recipe with a handful of ingredients.

"Mom used to make salmon patties a lot," says Akira. "Seems simple enough."

"Cool. Text your dad and tell him this evening's menu."

Mark texts her back: "Do you know how to take the bones out of canned salmon? It's messy. You might want to cook something else instead."

Akira's eyes cloud.

Wow! This guy really knows how to make his daughter feel like an idiot. "Tell Dad that at 26-years-old, you are fully capable of removing the bones."

She follows my instruction.

Finally, all systems are go.

Akira and I shop for ingredients to make salmon patties. Before I know what hits me, Akira has whizzed through Harris Teeter, a high-end grocery store. The gigantic structure is under construction, so the store is fairly empty. Bread crumbs. Eggs. Twenty-ounce can of salmon. Onion.

Ten minutes later, we're at the checkout counter. I'm poised to help with her debit card, but she slides the card through the reader just fine. I follow as she negotiates her shopping cart out the sliding door and through the parking lot.

"It's obvious you can do a lot of things on your own."

Akira stops and looks at me. "All I needed was for someone to believe in me."

I am humbled.

I stand beside Akira at her kitchen counter, reading aloud from the salmon patty recipe while she completes each step. The Stone family has every size measuring cup, baking pan, oven cookware, mixing bowl, and mixer imaginable. I mentally review the meager handful of cooking items I have at home.

Akira mixes all the salmon patty ingredients together and pops them in the frying pan. "Annie was always the one who got to cook and bake with Mom."

"How did you feel about that?"

Akira shrugs. "I was too clumsy, anyway."

I suggest Akira clean as she goes, but she chooses to postpone that task until the patties are cooked. The kitchen counters are a mess, so she gives them a once-over. I sigh, and then demonstrate how to thoroughly wipe down the stove and counters.

Akira may have a devil-may-care attitude on cleaning the stove, but she's right on task when it comes to sweeping the floor. "I have to make sure Misty doesn't get into any random onion bits. Onions are toxic for dogs."

Mark's daughter isn't as oblivious as he assumes!

Akira fries a 'tester' patty for me. "Yum!" I say.

She grins. "Mission accomplished."

I high-five her. "Your dad will be thrilled."

Akira's smile reaches her eyes. "If I could do this, imagine what else I could be capable of in the kitchen. Let's try to cook something trickier next time."

"Sounds like a plan!"

I leave for home with a pleasantly filled tummy and a warm, fuzzy feeling.

The following week, Akira suggests we make chicken and fried rice. This time she's got all the ingredients.

I supervise as she cuts the chicken into cubes. Akira is nervous to use one of her dad's new knives to cut the chicken. "He actually cut a small sliver of skin off his thumb and warned me to be careful. My hands tremble. Sometimes they shake to the point I can't hold things properly."

Fortunately, she manages to cut the chicken without adding bits of body parts into the mix. Once everything is mixed together, we add the soy sauce. It takes a few taste tests before we agree the fried rice has enough zing to it.

Delicious. Akira can now add fried rice to her recipe accomplishments. "How do you think you did today?" I ask.

Akira performs a little victory dance. "If anything, cooking a trickier dish built up my confidence and self-esteem. Now I have things other than grilled cheese and TV dinners I can prepare for me and Dad."

Pet Sitting Business

Once again, I sit across from Akira and her dad. "Akira needs to earn her own money to buy personal grooming items. It's time for us to revisit the pet sitting business idea. You ready, kiddo?"

Akira's eyes sparkle. "Sounds like fun!"

Mark, however, is ambivalent. "I'd still really prefer Akira to have regular income coming in."

"Noted," I say. "But with no car, she needs to do something local to bring in money. She can add this experience to her resume."

It takes a while, but Mark finally acquiesces.

The next day, Akira designs a computer-generated flyer and business cards for her pet sitting business.

I'm impressed. "No way could I design computer-generated business cards."

"Honestly, it's not that hard. Just a game controller image in the corner with a blue and purple background."

We search the internet for pet-themed images. Akira finds an adorable clip-art of a dog and cat sitting side by side. "It makes sense to include both animals on the card because this will create more pet sitting opportunities," she says.

Wow! This gal is right on the mark.

I remain silent as Akira re-sizes the clipart and pastes it on the bottom of the flyer. After she types in her contact and service fee information, we develop a two-sentence script for her to say when she rings a neighbor's bell:

> Hi, my name is Akira Stone. I live down the street from you. I just started my own pet sitting/walking service. Here's my flyer and card.

"Great. Now you're going to place the flyer on the front porch of each house," I instruct her.

Akira has that deer-in-the-headlights expression. "My neighborhood doesn't allow solicitation."

"Is there a sign that says so?"

"No," she says nervously, "but people will get mad at me."

"You live here, and you're offering to watch their dogs and cats at only twenty-five dollars per day while they're on vacation. How is that a bad thing?"

Akira picks at a dried skin patch on her cheek. "Two months ago, a neighbor was robbed because she left newspapers on her front porch while she was on vacation."

"No problem. If no one answers the door when you knock, you can leave the flyer between the door and the screen door."

Akira remains dubious.

"Don't worry. I'll stand beside you as you knock on the doors." This is a big deal for me to promise, as each one-acre house has a driveway big enough to accommodate ten cars. I'm in good physical condition, but August in North Carolina is a scorcher.

Akira gives me a tentative smile.

We step outside onto her front porch. "Today we are going to drop off twenty-five flyers."

Akira blanches, probably thinking it would be difficult to pull off in this sweltering heat. "I don't have the stamina to walk to twenty-five different houses."

Perhaps I am being a bit demanding. "Let's just give it a shot and see how far we get."

She nods, relieved.

Together, we hoof our way down Akira's block, house after house. Sweat pours down our brows as we power-walk up the blur of driveways.

I stand next to Akira as she rings bell after bell and spouts her two-sentence spiel. She speaks softly despite my whispering in her ear to speak louder, but the homeowners do listen politely. Her hands tremble as she gives each homeowner a pet sitting flyer. A couple of neighbors indicate interest. I encourage Akira to write down their contact information.

She pooh-poohs my suggestion. "I'll remember. I don't need to write it down."

After distributing six flyers, Akira is ready to call it quits. I mentally file *persistence* as another trait we need to work on. Then I proceed to negotiate. "Nine more flyers and we'll be done for today."

Akira reluctantly nods.

We cut through the yard of one of the homes to get to the next street over. Then onto the next street as we navigate our way down a forest path with lots of twists and turns. Who knew Akira and I would get lost this close to her house?

The answer is obvious. Akira doesn't walk, jog, or bike. This is one of the few times Akira has actually traversed her immediate area by foot in the eleven years her family has lived here.

"How do we get back?" I ask.

"If we can make our way to the main road, we can figure out our way home," she says.

Good reasoning, I mentally note.

Surprisingly, we arrive back at her house in little time. Autistic folks tend to become anxious when even the tiniest change occurs, but Akira is calm as a hibernating bear. *Does her logic, reasoning, and lack of anxiety indicate a possible misdiagnosis?* I wonder.

Dripping with sweat, we stomp up her front stairs.

Akira unlocks the door. "That's enough walking for me."

Once inside, she gives me a glass of water without request.

Together we chug ice-cold glasses of water. "You did a good job, kiddo. A lot of your neighbors seemed interested. How do you feel about all you accomplished today?"

Akira's eyes glow. "I'm tired, sweaty, and thirsty, but we accomplished my goal for the week. I'm honestly impressed with how well I did. I thought for sure I wouldn't get a single interested person, let alone be able to walk as far as I did."

"You looked them right in the eye when you spoke," I marvel.

She snickers. "That wasn't easy. I was even more impressed that I was able to converse with neighbors I didn't know well."

"You kept going, even though it was boiling outside."

"That's because you wouldn't let me quit," she teases. "Handing out twenty-five flyers next week won't be as tough, because I built up some physical stamina today. Walking gave me some much-needed exercise."

"Your sense of direction is amazing. You didn't freak out when we got lost."

Akira nods. "Guess I'm not as dumb as I thought. I really hope I get some clients from this adventure."

Success! God enabled me to remove one iota of Akira's security blanket today.

Pet Sitting Boot Camp

WHEN AKIRA AGREED TO charge me $25 per day to sit my three small dogs, I jumped at the chance to be her first customer and booked her on the spot.

My hubby initially worried about how an inexperienced dog sitter would manage three dogs, so we started with a three-day weekend to visit my daughter in Florida. I was just glad to be on the road. Besides, Akira and my doggies are good buddies.

Upon our return, Akira admitted her dad had to come and help her clean the carpets where the dogs had peed and pooped.

"No more road trips," said my hubby, but I assured him Akira would improve with experience. Everybody deserves a second chance, and no way was I going to pass up a second vacation reservation!

This time, only a handful of pee spots were visible upon our return.

By our third trip, Akira was paying more attention to the dogs than to her laptop computer. More walks, more cuddles. Only two potty accidents.

Together, Akira and I have worked it out through trial and error. We were both motivated to make it work, and we did.

Now Akira has a good idea of how to pet sit.

Sure enough, later that week, Akira received her second pet sitting client—a neighbor who responded to her flyer.

DMV Test Failure

I'm freaking out," says Akira. "Even though I've driven the course with my driving teacher and my dad enough times I know it by heart, I still don't feel ready."

In route to another tutoring student's house, I listen to Akira over Bluetooth. "You'll do fine. Just do your deep breathing and visualization exercises before beginning the road test."

This is Akira's second try. We've been working on meditation and visual imagery, helpful techniques to relieve anxiety. Hopefully it works in the upcoming stressful situation.

"I got honked at because I didn't know I could make a right turn on a red light."

"But now you do know. Good luck. You'll do fine."

As I click off the call, I reflect on Mark's ambivalent attitude toward his daughter getting her driver's license. On one hand, he wants her to get a job. On the other hand, he's concerned she'll have a panic attack if another car shoots in front of her or if she misses an exit. These are valid concerns every parent shares, but voicing those concerns aloud to one's child only creates anxiety and stress.

A couple of hours later, I phone Akira. "How did it go?"

Akira's voice sounds teary. "Not so great."

"What happened?"

Akira blurts out the story. "Dad and I drove to the DMV and parked. I was worried I'd hit someone while I was trying to find a parking spot. Dad assured me that I'd be fine. We walked into the testing center and I pulled a number.

"When it was my turn, a large woman came and got me. We walked out to my car, a blue Toyota Camry, which originally was Mom's, and I got inside. The proctor had me use the turn signals, hazard lights, and honk the horn to show the car was in working condition. I panicked because she was a rather strict instructor.

"The proctor told me a turn was coming up. When somebody snaps at me, I tend to make more mistakes. I overshot the first turn and almost hit a street sign.

"Her voice got harsh. She said, 'Are you trying to kill us? You completely missed that turn. Back up and go again.'

"I did as she said, only to have a car barrel around the corner as I was backing up. Yet again, the proctor snapped at me. I felt like breaking into tears. Dad was watching, too.

"I rapidly apologized to her, and she told me the test was over. I would have to try again in several months. Apparently when you almost kill the proctor you have to wait to take it again.

"I slumped my way back to Dad. I told him I had failed and that I wanted him to drive home. I was near tears at this point and didn't have the self-esteem to drive anywhere after that. The minute I got to my room I broke into water works."

"At least you tried," I say. "Were you nervous because your dad was watching?"

"Yes."

"Next time I'll come with you and you'll pass, you'll see."

"If I bomb again, I won't be able to continue down the path we all set."

"We just need to role-play the road test scenario, that's all."

I pray I am correct.

Volunteering

I'M BIG INTO VOLUNTEERING. Even as an eight-year-old child growing up in Chicago, I felt a kinship with children in need. I made my mom take me to synagogue, where we talked to the board members about starting a Toys for Tots program. They turned my idea down. That program was still a twinkle in somebody else's eye. In that same time frame, President Kennedy was telling Americans to "Ask not what your country can do for you. Ask what you can do for your country."

One day my mom received a mailer from the Cystic Fibrosis Foundation, asking for monetary donations for medical research. Not much was known about this disease that lead to death before age ten and caused lungs to fill with mucus. I felt sorry for these kids.

My own childhood was shaky. I shared a one-bedroom apartment with my divorced mom, who worked a million hours a week. But, it was a lot worse for these kids. The least I could do was go door-to-door on my block, taking donations.

These days, living in the city is a lot more transient. People move in and out of apartment buildings. Homeowners greet their neighbors with "Hi" and "Bye" as they drive off to work. The next-door neighbor could be a pedophile, and you wouldn't know it unless you researched it.

I'm not surprised to learn that in Akira's younger years, her autism took up way too much space in the family for anybody to bring up the subject of volunteerism.

It wasn't until her mid-teens that Akira volunteered as a teacher's assistant at her temple's religious school program. She helped with the lessons and distributed snacks.

Part of my life-coaching plan is to introduce Akira to volunteering in the community, so I phone to invite her to feed the homeless with me tonight.

"I'm sleeping," she whispers.

"At 3:30 in the afternoon?"

"I feel like crap after failing the driving test, and I'm not leaving the comfort of my bedroom."

Tough love time. "I am so sorry, kiddo. Volunteering will get your mind off everything."

"I can't drive," she moans.

A driver's license symbolizes freedom, independence, a job, a social life. Without it, you're talking prisoner in silk handcuffs. "I'll drive you. We're just going to serve food to 120 homeless people at the First Presbyterian Church."

"What if I drop the lemonade pitcher? You know I have a tremor."

The word *excuse* is not in my vocabulary, nor will I allow it to be in hers. "If you spill, we'll mop it up. Besides, they have food trays, too."

"I don't know," she cries.

"Look, you have done great with every challenge I've thrown at you so far."

"But this is a mountainous task. How am I supposed to pass out food to an auditorium full of strangers?"

"Together with me, that's how," I reassure her.

Akira may have failed her driver's test today, but tonight, she is going to be a super star. I feel it in my gut. My no excuses, take no prisoners activism is the tough love Akira needs.

Two hours later, we hightail past a couple dozen homeless folks already waiting outside the church. We knock on the glass door and a volunteer lets us into the building. I glance at Akira. She looks petrified. "What's wrong?"

"I'm still not sure I can do this," she says shakily.

"It's normal to feel unsure in a new situation. You can do this. Just breathe."

"I'm nervous as hell."

"My advice to you is take your mind off yourself and focus on helping somebody else."

"That's easier said than done," she says, miserably.

I take her arm and we grab nametags before joining the circle of volunteers. The woman running the Hot Dish for Hope event asks if any of us is a first timer. Akira hesitantly raises her hand, along with a few other volunteers. We each say our name and the temple/church we are from.

The church facilitator reviews house rules. Then each of us is appointed to take various stations: pouring drinks, preparing food plates, wheeling food carts into the dining hall, serving the food, and cleaning up. Ten minutes later, homeless individuals and families stream into the dining hall and, after a short speech and grace by the church pastor, are fed.

"Akira, could you go around and pour people drinks?" the person in charge asks.

I watch as she puts one hand beneath the pitcher to keep it steady. Better safe than sorry.

Akira smiles hesitantly as she circulates throughout the room, pouring lemonade for eight people per table. Soon she's gone through three pitchers.

A few clients comment on her work and say they would be happy to have her serve them. Beaming at the compliment, Akira says, "I hope you enjoy the meal. It should be out soon."

The meal consists of chicken, veggies, mashed potatoes, and a bread roll. It takes two volunteers to distribute the food; one volunteer holds the tray and the other gives each person a plate of food.

The volunteers, Akira, and I continue to walk around the room, refilling drinks. A few times Akira refills our pitchers.

When the meal is over, we volunteers help ourselves to the remaining food. It is a nice gesture, and Akira and I fill our plates. "After working non-stop for over an hour, I was rather hungry," she says

"Did you enjoy serving?"

"A warm meal is always welcome," she says brightly. "Just because it's free doesn't make it any less special to the people who come."

I chuckle to myself. Free is exactly the reason all these people *do* come.

We finish eating, thank the woman in charge, and stroll out to the car. "So how did you like volunteering?"

"I'm in a better mood now since I helped a large number of people," she says.

In Hebrew, we call it *Tzedakah*—an act of charity. "It took a lot of guts for you to go to an event you knew nothing about and feed a hundred and twenty strangers."

Akira grins. "It sure beats sitting home, feeling sorry for myself. I actually enjoyed myself. I didn't even spill the pitcher or make a fool of myself. I feel like I can take on just about anything now."

On our ride home, Akira's body language exudes self-confidence.

"You did a good deed tonight."

Akira nods. "But it was nerve-wracking."

I pull into her driveway. "Just remember there are always people who are worse off than you. Plus, you overcame your fear."

"Maybe." She opens the passenger door, then turns to face me.

"Forget something in the car?" I ask.

Akira shakes her head. "After you came to our house that first time, I joined a Skype call with my boyfriend Damon, who lives in the Netherlands."

My eyes widen. "I don't recall you ever mentioning him."

"We've been together seven years and counting. I told him you were going to be my life coach, to help me become more independent and fill the hole left by Mom. I was a bit unsure about the situation."

It's been a long day for both of us. I wonder why Akira is sharing these little gems just as I'm about to drive off. Now my curiosity won't allow me to leave. "What's Damon like?"

"He's funny. He's on the autism spectrum, and he's a dishwasher."

A little bird tells me Daddy must not be thrilled with the young man's ability to support his daughter someday.

Akira continues. "From the moment Mom was sent to hospice to the moment she passed, Damon has been my shoulder to cry on. He even was there for the five years Mom went through chemo. Even though we live in different countries, he is always there for me."

I shut off the ignition and face her. "It's wonderful to have someone in your life who really gets you."

Akira beams.

"So how did Damon react when you told him about me?"

"He asked if you knew I was autistic. I said, 'Yes, but she doesn't believe Dad about the diagnosis.' Then I turned on the camera and mimicked the wide-eyed, are-you-serious face you see in TV dramas. This got Damon laughing, and he turned on his camera, as well."

Her description of their conversation makes me grin. However, I am still clueless about why she requires my presence at this moment.

"Suddenly, Pepper, Damon's black and white Persian mixed cat, was staring at me. Damon jokingly pitched his voice to make it higher. 'I am the pepper cat, and you shall obey my cuteness!'

"We talked for a few more hours until Damon fell asleep. He actually dozed off on his keyboard, snoring and mumbling in Dutch. Having talked to him about what might happen during your testing helped a little."

Seriously? I've just missed watching the new TV episode of *The Goldbergs* so she can chat about her boyfriend? Attempting to stifle my annoyance, I'm just about to tell her I'm leaving when she starts to tear up. Immediately my annoyance changes to concern. "What's wrong, Sweetie?"

"Next to Damon, you are the one other person in my life who

doesn't think I'm an idiot. You challenge me to be the best person I can be. You make me believe I deserve to be happy."

My jaw drops. I throw my arms around her. "You are worth fighting for, Akira."

This moment definitely overrides TV.

Opening Up

AKIRA AND I OFTEN lunch at my house before beginning our coaching sessions. As we nibble on grilled cheese sandwiches, my client's deepest emotions reveal themselves.

At this moment, we are discussing her childhood, a topic she's been reticent to delve into during past sessions.

"When I was a kid, I was a real handful. I almost wasn't allowed to go to pre-school at age four because I refused to get out of diapers. My pediatrician diagnosed me with high-functioning autism. Back in the 1990s, being autistic was considered retardation. Teachers and other parents felt bad for my mom and dad. Many times, things I did, like obsessing over Pokémon cards at age fourteen, were not considered age appropriate, and the kids who found out would tell my sister."

I sip my lemon water. "How would your sister react?"

"Annie would nag and complain to me about how I should act more like the other kids. I thought I was acting normal."

It is emotionally painful to be the sibling of a child with special needs. Sibs may shut down, act out, or wind up parenting the parents. Of course, they can also direct their hunger for attention into a positive goal, like achieving excellence in academics, sports, or the arts.

"What kind of inappropriate-aged activities are we talking about?" I ask.

"My retarded antics, as Annie called them, started long before high school. When I was six years old, I was playing helicopter in the den with a piece of silly putty stuck to the end of a string. I lost my balance and bashed my chin on the edge of the metal bookcase. I cried like crazy from the pain and was bleeding badly. I had to go to the hospital and get stitches."

"That could happen to any kid. What else?"

"When I was eight, my family and I were visiting my grandparents in Texas during summer vacation. I thought it would be fun to try jumping from Grandpa's armchair, over the coffee table, onto the couch. I misjudged the jump and smacked the back of my head on the coffee table as I landed on the couch. I had to get stitches again."

"You were inquisitive. Perfectly normal. What else?"

Akira gives me a sideways glance. "Then there were the many heated arguments between my younger sister and me. Arguments about what ride to go on at the amusement park. Even arguments about who got the last pancake."

I huff. "There is nothing retarded about how you acted."

Akira raises her eyebrows. "But I was getting negative attention, not positive."

Been there, done that. When I was in eighth grade, my mom worked full-time. I would always act up in after-school Pom Poms class in order to get my teacher's attention. Then there was the time I put a goldfish into my social studies teacher's water glass for April Fool's Day. "What else?"

"When I was ten, I attended summer camp. Every morning, the campers sang the Israeli national anthem. I asked my counselor if I could sing a song. He agreed and let me go up on the platform.

"I proudly belted out Cruella Deville from *101 Dalmatians*, word for word, to about two hundred people. Either I was extremely brave or extremely stupid."

"You loved to sing and perform. How is that a bad thing?"

Akira looks at me, disbelieving. "On another occasion, Christopher, my favorite toy rabbit, was dropped in a muddy rain puddle. A counselor jokingly said I should clean him like a mother cat. I licked the rabbit and ended up sick!"

"Okay, that was a bit weird," I admit.

Akira sends me an *I told you so* glance.

"I continued to act retarded until sixth grade when Mom finally put me through pragmatics classes. A psychiatrist worked with a group of four to six young clients. He taught us everything from how to talk to strangers at social gatherings to how to pick up on sarcasm and facial expressions.

"The classes helped me curb stomp my social mishaps. I admit these classes didn't fix me, like my classmates or my sister expected. But they did help me figure out if my actions were ones that would make people treat me as if I were retarded."

"How did your parents respond through all of this?"

"Through all these years, through every accident and adventure, Mom was there for me. She would comfort me when I was upset and cheered her lungs out during my equestrian competition. I won a red ribbon in vaulting and a purple ribbon in the obstacle course."

Chalk one up for Akira. "Sounds like you could really depend on your mom."

Akira shrugs. "I guess. When I was twenty-one, Mom got diagnosed with ovarian cancer. Despite being on chemo, she still found the energy to drive me to college classes, cook dinner, and feed the dog. She was a fighter through and through.

"She coined a new term for her forgetfulness: chemo brain. This term stuck and enabled us to laugh during nerve-racking months of chemo treatments. I'm honored to have had a loving mother like her. If I ever have children, I will raise them with as much love as she gave me."

As I sweep the crumbs from the table, I muse on how lucky Akira was to have had at least one family member fighting for her.

Driver's Test: Round Three

IT'S BEEN TWO MONTHS since Akira's last attempt at passing the driver's exam and we're on the way to the DMV for a retake. Hopefully, this is her lucky day. I park my car in Akira's driveway and slip into the passenger's side of her mom's Camry. "Nice car!"

"When I drive Mom's car, it reminds me of all the good times I shared with her. I even nicknamed the car Selene, which was Mom's middle name. By the way, are you okay with me driving?"

"Sure," I say. "Why do you ask?"

"When I drove, Mom or Dad was in the car with me. The closest testing center is a fifteen-minute drive."

I suppress a grin. As a Chicago native, I would boast, "My office is only fifteen minutes from home!" But a North Carolinian would lament, "My office is fifteen minutes from home."

"I can't believe I failed so badly last time," she says. "I shouldn't have let that proctor's attitude get to me."

"That was then, this is now." Frankly, I'm more concerned about sitting in the passenger seat while Akira navigates the road.

"When you have autism, being yelled at makes you want to curl up in a ball or shut down completely."

"Nobody's going to yell at you this time." *Why is she glancing at her GPS instead of putting it on speaker?* I say nothing so she can concentrate on the road.

We pull into the DMV's tiny parking lot. I hear a slight tap, but Akira doesn't notice. I don't want to spook her before her road test, so I delete the sound from my mind.

Akira put her mom's car in park and beeped the lock button three times for good luck. Then we walk into the DMV and head for the check-in counter.

Akira's behind-the-wheel exam is scheduled for ten a.m., and we've arrived right on the dot. Without my coaching her on how to proceed, Akira whips out her learner's permit, as well as a do/don't list of criteria on how to effectively interact with people with autism. "My mom made this card for me before she died," she says.

The woman peruses the caveats on the I Have Autism card:

> I Have Autism. I may panic if yelled at, misinterpret tasks you ask me to do, or not be able to answer your questions.

The woman smiles. "We have the perfect proctor for you, Ms. Stone."

The woman told Akira to pull a ticket from the machine next to the counter. "This reminds me of the deli at the grocery store," Akira says. "Only this is the DMV, and I'm not here to order roast beef."

"Focus, Akira," I say. "You need to pass this time, not think about food."

The woman disappears into another room. Minutes later, she returns with a tall, stocky, middle-aged man.

"I heard about what happened with your last proctor," he says, smiling down at Akira. "Don't worry. I'm not strict like she was. We'll get you that license yet."

Akira and I smile at each other.

The proctor writes down Akira's car model and license plate number. I take him aside for a moment. "Akira failed a previous test. We need her to pass this time."

He gives me an understanding nod. Then he and Akira head out the door.

Like the last attempt, she is asked to honk the horn, turn on the hazards, and flash the turn signals. She does each of these while he stands in front of the car.

"Everything appears to be in working order, Akira," he says getting in the passenger seat. Akira has phoned me prior to getting inside, so I am able to hear what's going on.

"Now just pull out of the parking lot slow and easy," the proctor says calmly. "I'm not going to rush you."

"I'm going slow because the parking lot is packed like a barrel of monkeys and I don't want to hit anything," she says.

"That's fine. Okay, we're coming to a turn."

Akira's voice sounds tremulous. "I fishtailed the last time I got to this turn."

"You'll do fine. Just take deep breaths and relax."

A few seconds later, I hear, "I did it! I thought for sure I would mess up again. Can we take a minute for me to catch my breath?"

"Of course," he replies. "We're in no rush, Akira."

She takes a few deep breaths before indicating that they can continue with the rest of the driving test.

"I need you to drive down to the black mailbox and do a three-corner turn."

"You can do it," he says. Then a few seconds later, "Good job, Akira. Now I want you to drive backward as straight as you can." A few seconds later: "Perfect."

"Slam the accelerator and then come to a stop as safely as you can," he directs.

"Great job. You can drive back to the parking lot. The test is complete."

I watch them come through the side door. My face holds a question mark.

Akira shoots me a thumbs up and a goofy grin. "Victory!"

"Congratulations." I give Akira a bear hug. The opportunities this success will bring her are enormous.

Akira fills out the information for her driver's license. "I still can't believe I got my license. And it only took me three tries."

The proctor tells her it will take two weeks for her new license to arrive. "That's quick," she says. "I'll be able to drive to work or the grocery store on my own. No more having to listen to NPR every time I get in the car with Dad. I get to pick the radio station I want."

I walk over to the tester. He is completing Akira's paperwork. "Thanks so much for helping her," I say.

He leans across his desk. "She narrowly passed the parallel parking and backing up sections of the test. She needs to practice pulling in and out of parking spaces."

I glance at Akira. She's across the room, posing for her driver's license photo. "No problem," I say gaily. At this moment, we both need to revel in this dizzying feeling of success.

Akira proudly positions her new license in her new turquoise wallet. After sharing a celebratory lunch, we make our way back to the parking lot.

We are discussing our plans for the rest of the afternoon when we notice two young men, no older than Akira, standing next to the white car parked adjacent to hers.

"Is the Camry yours?" one of them asks.

Akira nods.

He points to her front bumper and then to his back bumper.

Akira pales. "My car tapped yours," she says.

I explain she had just taken her driver's test. "Neither of us realized she'd tapped your car." My statement is at least fifty-percent accurate.

They exchange insurance information, and the owner of the other vehicle calls the police to file an accident report.

Akira begins to breathe heavily. "Dad's going to be so pissed at me."

I murmur reassuringly, "It's going to be okay."

By the time the officer arrives, Akira is shaking.

"I need your insurance card, miss," he tells her.

Akira opens her wallet and hands the officer her health insurance card.

"Your car insurance card, not your health insurance card."

"Look in your glove compartment," I suggest.

Akira locates the card; it has expired.

Akira is so scared that her voice comes out in a whisper. "I'll call my dad and have him come meet us here."

"You don't need to do that, Akira," I counsel. "Just text your dad and ask for the name and phone number of your car insurance company."

"It's not in my name. This was my mom's car before she died."

"Your dad must have you listed as a driver on your mom's car," I say.

"I don't know. I better have Dad come."

"You could," I continue, "but you're almost twenty-seven years old, and it's important for you to learn how to handle these things on your own."

Akira looks dubious.

"These things happen all the time, especially when you're a new driver," I say.

"She's right," says the officer. "Your insurance deductible probably will cover this one."

Akira phones her dad to get the information. A minute later, she clicks off the phone and begins picking at dry skin on her arms. "Dad says he's on his way here. He's furious I created a basketball-sized dent on the front bumper of my car. The other car only has minor scratches, which still require a new paint job."

We're all sweating by the time Mark arrives. "Akira, what did you do?" he snaps.

"I know you're ticked off to be dragged from work for this, but I had no clue how to file a claim myself," she says softly.

Mark gives the two men their insurance information and then helps them file the report on the cars. Once the claim is completed, he drives off without a backward glance.

Akira puts her head in her hands. "This was not how I expected getting my driver's license would turn out."

We head to my car. "Don't beat yourself up about the accident. You successfully dealt with the situation and learned another life lesson in doing so."

Akira slips into the passenger seat and gives me the tiniest of smiles. "Maybe."

Twenty minutes later, I pull into her driveway. Akira whispers goodbye and slams the door behind her.

As I pull away from the curb, I castigate myself for expecting Akira to handle the insurance situation without her dad's on-the-spot assistance; no way did she have the knowledge or the emotional strength to do so.

It takes so much effort to teach someone how to handle the everyday ins and outs of life. I am still teaching my own kids how to cope with life's unexpected occurrences. There is no way to plan for every single contingency. All we can do is instruct our young people on who to call in emergencies, encourage them to keep their documentation handy, and drum it into their heads to be aware of their surroundings for safety issues.

A good reminder to us all.

Car Accident Number Two

Akira's second accident occurs days later in McDonald's parking lot. I'm meeting her for ice cream. My client has received her temporary driver's license; her hard copy version will arrive in the mail within the next couple of days.

12:00 p.m. Cars shoot in and out of the microscopic parking lot. I stand in front of her car and pantomime in which direction she needs to steer, but Akira is having trouble squeezing her Camry into the last available spot. She backs up several times before finally shutting off the ignition. Even then, her car is parked at an odd angle.

Once inside the restaurant, Akira peers out the window. "I'm not sure jamming my car into that parking space was a good idea. I'm afraid I'll get dinged. Maybe we should leave."

My ADHD kicks in. "Our *free ice cream* coupons expire tonight. I'll order fast."

Akira gazes out the window. "Not hungry."

Once I finish my ice cream, we walk out to the parking lot and she slips into her car.

Since I've driven my own car to the restaurant, I have no idea how tightly packed in her car actually is. I attempt to navigate her out.

Bonk.

Akira gets out to check. "I'm screwed!" she laments.

This time her front right bumper has grazed another car; a few scratches are the only damage. I run inside to find the car's owner; she's a McDonald's employee. We phone the police. Akira apologizes profusely since she has only recently gotten her car repaired from the previous accident.

I tell Akira to phone her dad and tell him what happened. "This time, I will fill out the claim myself," she tells him.

Mark balks, but Akira holds her ground. "If I'm going to have my own car, I need to know the ins and outs of owning one. This is one of the outs."

This time, Mark agrees not to come to the rescue; he says he will leave it in her hands.

It ends up taking an hour for the police to arrive. Akira and the other driver exchange information and take pictures of the damage. Before the officer leaves, he gives Akira a case number and instructs her to look online for the accident report, which is yet to be uploaded.

Together, we watch him leave. "Bravo. You handled the situation really well this time."

"This time I understood what I had to do, and I didn't freak out and stress as much," says Akira, "but I still feel bad that I caused another accident."

"Like the police officer told you last time, this stuff happens to new drivers all the time. But you learn from your mistakes."

Akira grins. "I did my best to make it easier for both myself and the other driver. I don't think I would have been able to do this if you weren't helping me to mature over the past three months."

I give Akira a bear hug, humbled by her acknowledgment of what we've been able to accomplish together. "What did you learn from our little adventure?"

She laughs. "From now on, I'm going to park far away from the next car!"

High Holidays Approaching

Rosh Hashanah, the Jewish New Year, is one week away. This sacred week also happens to be the one-year anniversary of Akira's mother's death. I am scheduled to sing in the Temple for High Holy Days.

"Did your family have people for Rosh Hashanah when your mom was alive?" I ask Akira.

"Back in Massachusetts, Mom always used to talk about how she'd like to hold a dinner for one of the holidays," says Akira. "We never got around to actually doing this. Our family didn't have many close friends. We also lived fifteen minutes away from the Temple, which was kind of far."

Again with the fifteen minutes. Give me a break!

Rocco and I recently moved to North Carolina and really don't know anyone well enough to invite them over for the holidays. We have been invited to a congregant's home for the second night. Holiday celebrations should be shared (think Easter brunch). However, we will be eating alone the first night—a real bummer. "Tell me about one close family friend."

Akira considers her answer. "That would have to be Leah and her family. Leah was the stereotypical high-functioning autistic young adult. She focused on Broadway musicals in particular and wouldn't talk about anything else. She didn't make eye contact, and she was extremely quiet."

I glance at my client sheepishly; her friend was exactly the type of person I expected to meet four months ago when I banged the brass knocker on the Stone's front door.

Akira continues. "Leah's family left the Temple after the rabbi wouldn't allow their daughter to continue singing solos in the choir."

Her last statement perks my attention. "Because she was autistic?"

Akira shakes her head. "Because her mom was a stage mom, always pushing for Leah to sing the main parts."

My thoughts return to Rosh Hashanah. I wonder if Akira realizes the impact of sharing these High Holiday meals. Why should she? Her mother would have organized these rituals. Now it's just her, her sister, and her father.

I have a couple of alternatives up my sleeve for that lonely first night. I can invite the Stone family to my house for dinner, or Akira can host her first dinner party.

Personally, I prefer the second alternative. Even back in Chicago, my husband tired of hosting these annual dinners. He'd given me an ultimatum about hosting future events. But now that we are in North Carolina, I am seriously considering whether to override his veto. Before coming down like Attila the Hun, though, I will seek compromise, i.e., attempting to adhere to my husband's desire to go elsewhere for the holidays. If that means going to my student's house, so be it.

"Would you like to come to our house for Rosh Hashanah, or

would you prefer to host your own dinner at your house?" I ask.

I assume Akira will be reticent to host her own dinner party. I imagine having to twist her arm. *Am I any different from her sister?* I wonder.

Akira, however, chooses option number two, catching me off-guard. "If we are going to do this like Mom had wanted, our place will be best."

I recover quickly. "You can make the main dish and ask your guests to each bring something."

Akira's voice rises in excitement. "Mom would make a brisket every year. If anything would make it feel like Mom was here, a brisket would be it."

"Sounds fabulous," I say. I can almost taste the savory brisket of beef my own mother cooked for the High Holidays.

Akira's face falls. "I'm not sure if I could live up to Mom's delicious brisket; she always put Budweiser in the brisket. I better have Dad make it."

The year we married, Rocco wound up cooking the brisket because Mom's knee was giving her problems. He'd done it in secret while I'd been teaching school!

"Cook the brisket yourself," I recommend. "We'll do a trial run next week."

Success! My preferred choice of dining at Akira's house rather than my own isn't totally self-serving. When Akira hosts her first dinner party, her self-esteem will sky rocket. More importantly, her father and sister will view her as a young woman, not a teenager posing in a twenty-seven-year-old body.

"Are you okay with inviting a handful of folks from Temple whom neither of us know very well?" I ask tentatively.

"I guess," Akira replies. We come up with three names from our congregation: three of Akira's friends she hasn't talked to since high school, our family friend Ray, Rocco, my son Derek, and Akira's sister, Annie.

The only wild card is Akira's sister. According to Akira, Annie is all "rainbows and sunshine" with everybody except her. As Akira scales one mountain after another, her sister follows, kicking her in the shins with nailed work boots.

Mark fails to step in between his two daughters when the cutthroat sparring begins. There is no reason to think this night will be any different.

I'm apprehensive Annie will hijack her sister's dinner party. Then again, she might boycott it instead. I'm not certain which outcome would be worse.

Akira, however, has more pressing concerns. "I should probably ask Dad what he thinks first, though."

"Don't ask," I counsel. "Tell him you'd like to do a dinner party. Ask for his thoughts on the subject."

"But it's his house," she protests.

I'm taken aback. "What do you mean? You've lived in this house for eleven years."

"Mom and Dad always told me this is their house."

"It's your house, too."

"Not really. I don't pay any rent."

"Do you think that when your mom died, she wanted you to be tossed out on your ear if you didn't pay rent?"

Akira looks pensive. "I don't know."

I stare at her. She truly is unsure. "She didn't. You're their daughter. This is your house, too."

Akira remains dubious.

I sigh. We are drifting into none-of-my-business land—not that this normally would stop me from offering my two cents worth. But this subject is definitely an Akira and her dad conversation. "Why don't you give your dad a call?"

Minutes later, Akira is beaming. Mark is down with Rosh Hashanah dinner at their house.

I need to coach my client on a potpourri of skills in preparation for the big day, including how to:

- invite guests,

- plan a dinner menu,

- request each guest to bring a side dish,

- confirm who's coming,

- shop for holiday food,

- cook the brisket,

- choose an appropriate outfit to wear,

- set the table,

- greet people as they come to the door,

- serve the meal,

- make conversation with guests during the meal,

- clear the table, and

- load the dishwasher.

We begin next week!

Holiday Dinner

THE WEEK FLIES BY. Akira completed each preparation step with no foul-up. The big day is here. Rocco and I arrive early. I give Akira a special Star of David necklace as a gift. She takes it and tells me her mother had given her a similar gift years before, but she'd misplaced it.

She does, however, neglect to say *Thank You.* I mentally file that tidbit for a future coaching session.

I'll also be devoting another lesson to not answering the door with wet, stringy hair!

The doorbell rings. Akira follows the script we created for greeting each guest. Her friends are in absentia and her sister has decided to boycott this evening's festivities.

At the dinner table, Akira follows my demonstration of how to pass the serving dishes. My matzo ball soup is a winner, as is Mark's barbecue. Akira leans over and whispers, "Dad and I spent the afternoon cooking brisket. We don't usually cook together. We don't usually do a lot together."

Although Akira didn't cook the brisket herself, it was obviously a great daddy-daughter bonding experience.

Carol's fruit kugel and Sarah's seven-layer salad are fantastic. Ray's delicious honey cake, cookies, and flowers add to the celebration.

Misty, Akira's dog, jumps on everyone, begging for attention. She attaches herself to my young adult son.

Conversation over dinner is light and carefree. We talk about yoga, vegetarian recipes, and sports. Akira does a good job of inserting her own anecdotes, usually about her sister or her mother. I lament she is never the protagonist of her own stories. Then, again, what can you talk about when, but for a ride to junior college, grocery store, or a restaurant, you've been homebound for seven years?

Tonight is a gold star event. The guests compliment Akira on a lovely evening as they make their way out the door.

When the last guest leaves, I pull Akira aside. "You were a star tonight."

She grunts her assent.

"How do you feel?"

"Like I just climbed Mt. Everest. Mom would have been proud. It felt like she was smiling down on us. She always wanted to do this and finally we did."

"You took a risk and you succeeded. I bet your dad is so proud of you."

"I don't know."

"Hang on a minute."

I join Mark in the kitchen. He is loading the dishwasher.

"Everybody had a great time. Akira did a bang-up job, didn't she?"

Mark just smiles.

"Think I can pull you away from the dishes so you can tell Akira how well she did?"

Mark follows me into the dining room. Akira is clearing the last of the drinking glasses from the table.

"Your dad has something to say to you."

Akira looks at him expectantly.

"Good job," he says softly. Then he disappears back into the kitchen.

"Okay, then. See how proud of you he is?"

"I guess."

"What do you mean? He just said so."

"It's hard to tell. Getting Dad to speak a full sentence about anything is not an easy task. At least he complimented me. That's a step in the right direction."

"If *you* are proud of you, that's what really matters."

Akira offers a tiny smile. "I was uneasy about inviting new people, but after meeting everyone and talking with them about Mom, I feel like I honored her memory tonight."

I hug her, collect my hubby and son, and bid the Stone family *L'Shana Tova*.

Happy New Year!

Learning to Speak at Toastmasters

It's October 2015, four months since I began coaching Akira. So far, my client has successfully confronted every challenge I've thrown her way. Now it's time for her to develop the ability to effectively communicate with others. In that spirit, I invite her to attend Toastmasters International, a hundred-year-old public speaking organization.

"Will there be a bunch of adults sitting around a table talking and having wine and cheese?" Akira asks.

"Not exactly. Have you ever spoken in front of a large group of people?"

"When my mom died, the rabbi asked me to share a few parting words. I was a stuttering mess. On the other hand, my sister expressed her thoughts as if she was accepting the Nobel Peace Prize."

No surprise there. Fear of public speaking originated in prehistoric times when early humans depended on one another for food and protection. Being ostracized, or expelled, from the group meant certain death.

"When you were young, did you play with other kids?" I ask. Not a strange question to ask of a person with autism.

Akira picks at a scab on her arm. "I played on my own a lot, or another kid and I would play together at opposite ends of the room. The most interaction I ever got was, 'Hand me that block.'"

"How did it go in high school?"

"I would tell other classmates that my brain was wired differently than theirs, but when I was asked to explain further, I drew a blank. It pained me not to be able to engage in everyday conversation. Since people couldn't understand how to interact with me, they either trampled on my words or treated me like I was less than human."

If seventy-four percent of people today fear speaking in public, imagine the social anxiety a person on the autism spectrum must experience. For that reason alone, you'd think I wouldn't subject Akira to the torture of learning how to speak in public.

You'd be wrong.

"Compassionate tough love" symbolizes my brand of life coaching. If Akira's dad wants her to eventually live independently, she needs to develop the necessary skills. Toastmasters is a microcosm of the real world, with a dash of empathy thrown in for extra flavor.

Akira and I trudge up the stairs to the Toastmasters meeting. "How do you feel?" I ask.

"Like I'm walking into the gates of hell. My body is sweating. I'm petrified about how everyone will treat me. How will they react to me having a life coach? Will they realize I'm autistic?"

"Those are all normal reactions people experience their first time entering a new group situation," I reassure her.

As we walk into the room, the group of ten members greets Akira with friendly smiles and words. The Toastmaster in charge of today's meeting explains the rules to Akira, but she looks shell-shocked. Observing what goes on will give her an idea of what to expect.

In Toastmasters, beginners like Akira are gently encouraged to share an icebreaker with the group, a three-minute biographical speech. Over the next several months—or years—a speaker delivers a series of five- to seven-minute speeches, each with a different theme. One speech might focus on organizing one's thoughts, while another speech might focus on using vocal variety rather than speaking in a monotone.

A beginning or advanced speaker can work toward achieving a Competent Communicator Certificate. Equally as beneficial is earning a Competent Leader Certificate for assuming various leadership roles at weekly club meetings.

My goal is for Akira to revel in the encouraging, non-judgmental attitude of our Toastmasters members while learning to communicate. Akira appears to be on board.

Hmm. Maybe not so much. At this very moment, she is clutching the table edge so tensely her knuckles are turning red, and all she is doing is standing up to say her name and tell how she heard about Toastmasters International.

Akira gratefully sits down, and we listen to the first speaker give his presentation. A short time later, she is called on by the table topics master to do a table topic, i.e., give an impromptu response to a question.

Akira shuffles up to the podium. Her hands grip the podium as if she is awaiting a death sentence instead of a friendly question.

Question: *What would you do if you had more hours in the day?*

She gives a slight smile. "I would spend more time with my dad. My dad is probably losing his hair right now trying to think of activities we could share. The only thing we do together is grocery shopping."

Akira receives quite a few laughs after mimicking her dad

ripping out his hair.

After the meeting is over, I congratulate Akira on her performance. "You spoke for two minutes with no cue cards!"

"My heart was pounding. I was just glad they didn't growl, 'What are you doing here?'"

"Aren't you the funny one," I say.

"I can't believe it. Me, Akira Stone, someone with zero experience in speaking in front of an audience, has just successfully given a two-minute speech. Well, not exactly zero experience."

"Oh?"

"I've been the dungeon leader in World of Warcraft for groups of twenty to forty players. I had to explain how to battle the boss and not tank the floor; tanking the floor is like tripping in hopscotch, except more painful."

"So you have no problem leading, as long as it's during an online game?"

Akira nods. "Behind a computer screen, I am fearless. In front of people? Not so much. If I join Toastmasters, will I ever reach that level of comfort?"

"Eventually. It will look good on your resume, too."

"Not that I have a job yet," she adds.

If I can teach Akira the skills necessary to achieve these certificates, they will inoculate her against her sister's constant put-downs and prove to her dad and herself that she is a capable human being.

Like the saying goes, Rome wasn't built in a day.

Job Search

Four years before I started life-coaching Akira, Sheri, a job coach from Autism to Work, began sending a slew of Akira's generic resumes to pet stores, movie theaters, Goodwill, and grocery stores—every single entry-level job she could find. This campaign produced a total of three interviews and zero job offers.

Akira confessed her dad gave the job coach permission to plaster the universe with her resumes without notifying her first. "Hell, half of them I didn't even know she had sent until I started getting these emails thanking me for applying but the company had found someone more qualified.

"It wasn't respectful of Sheri to go behind my back and send out job applications without my knowledge, even if my dad had given her permission to do so. I'm twenty-seven years old. I should have a say in where I ended up with my career. The two of them betrayed my trust."

Akira is so right. Just because someone has a special needs label attached to their name doesn't mean her opinions and thoughts are of no consequences. It's all about respect.

It is distressing that Akira failed to receive updated Excel sheets that listed dates, company contact information, and feedback. It is even more disconcerting that she didn't think to question her father or her job coach about why she had no say in a matter so integral to her life goals.

To be honest, even if Akira had a say, she probably would have deferred to her father. She says her sister's comments that she was worthless and nobody would hire her, coupled with her father's silence, contributed to her low self-esteem. Thus, she allowed family members to pull her strings.

I see two reasons for this disappointing outcome: 1) resumes were not tailored to each particular type of venue, and 2) Akira's interpersonal communication skills were not up to snuff.

Akira disagrees with reason number two. She claims she made good eye contact with the prospective employer, spoke clearly and loud enough, and used positive body language.

But I've noticed Akira tends to thrust her right shoulder forward and her left shoulder back, causing a slight twist of her upper torso when she speaks to someone. That twist says, "I feel insecure and I'm out of here." Even at Toastmasters, her voice comes across soft and tentative when answering questions and her hair still looks unkempt unless I remind her to wash it.

It is difficult for us to recognize how we come across to others in our everyday lives, especially when we're interviewing for a job. For a job applicant with autism or another disability, it's a double whammy because she stresses about not coming across as *normal*. Although Akira previously engaged in role playing and video taping of a mock interview, it's different in real time with a real potential boss.

"Did you ever have a job before?" I ask.

Akira nods. "I worked at Kohl's Department Store. Those little black security tags you see on the merchandise? Putting those annoying buggers on the clothes was my job. Not the most glamorous job, but hey, at least I wasn't on latrine duty for the army. No offence to anyone in the army."

Her sense of humor is another puzzle piece that doesn't fit autism. "Go on."

"I worked at Kohl's for two years before I got the axe. My hours dwindled from twenty hours to eight hours per week. My boss would regularly phone me to say I did not need to come into work.

"On one of my assigned work days, Mom told me to go back to bed since I likely wouldn't be going to work today. The next day, my boss phoned Mom to tell her I had missed work and that I was terminated. This stunned both of us, and we began to wonder if they had been waiting for me to screw up so that they could fire me."

"How did your work evaluations look?" I ask.

"My manager never even gave me an evaluation during the two years I was there. I can't even remember a time I was praised for doing my job or for tagging an entire section during my shift. Even my pay was less than minimum wage. I only earned $7.00 per hour when the minimum wage was $7.25 per hour. That's twenty-five cents less.

"Being terminated from Kohl's put a big red mark on my employment record. Mom, Dad, and Sheri all tried desperately to find a way to get me rehired so I could leave Kohl's of my own accord. This bit us in the butt."

"How so?"

"Every time one of us would turn in a new job application, something would happen. They first claimed to have never received the application. Then they claimed they lost it. We must have turned in five or six applications before deciding they wanted nothing to do with me."

"How did losing your job make you feel?"

"Losing the job at Kohl's was tough for me. Every time Sheri sent out my resume, I would pray that the employer would overlook Kohl's firing me. Out of the hundreds of applications sent out I had three job interviews."

"Where else did you interview at?"

"The first was at The Limited. They didn't hire me because I had little knowledge about fashion.

"The second interview was at a veterinary hospital as a kennel assistant. They told me I would have been hired but they found someone who was training to become a vet tech.

"The third interview was a phone call with PetSmart. I was confident I would get this job. I had volunteered at Friendly Pets over the summer before Mom's decline. I had plenty of knowledge about animals and how to care for them. I am still waiting to hear back from them."

"How have these experiences affected your self-esteem?"

"I felt like garbage. What did I do wrong? I was a hard worker, got along great with my coworkers, and came to work on time. Being terminated caused my confidence to plummet. It also didn't help that my sister verbally tortured me."

"What would she say?"

"The three most common sentences Annie threw at me were, 'You're lucky they even kept you two years. It wasn't even a real position. Even a monkey could do it.' Hearing her say these things hurt me emotionally. We were sisters. We were supposed to have each other's back, not stomp on the other person to feel superior."

I lean forward in my office chair and look Akira in the eye. "Do you realize a new Akira is beginning to emerge?"

"No," she murmurs, dabbing at her eyes.

Sometimes it's therapeutic to review all the successes one has recently experienced. "What about the job fair we attended? You memorized a two-sentence script and successfully used it when you visited each table to ask for job information.”

“Not so successfully,” she sniffles.

I snicker inside my head. *Successfully* is a euphemism. In truth, Akira mumbled two to three words at each vendor’s table. But at least it was a start.

“Then you took it upon yourself to seek out the on-site Game Stop store and ask about employment opportunities.”

“I guess.”

“And you’re actually earning pet sitting money from me and your neighbor. That’s got to be an ego boost.”

“I’m not very good at pet sitting yet.”

“Your comfort level will increase as you develop more experience. What’s your scariest challenge to date?”

Akira thinks for a minute. “My first Toastmasters speech when I briefly shared my autobiography. Xanax helped.”

Even with Xanax, she continues to grip the podium when she goes up to speak. But in Toastmasters, it isn’t how well a newbie comes across, it’s the fact that she actually rose to the occasion.

“You’re driving now,” I remind her.

“I am becoming more comfortable driving back and forth to Toastmasters and to our life-coaching sessions by myself,” she concedes. “But I’m still scared to drive at night or during a thunderstorm.”

“One step at a time, Akira.”

Our coaching session is over. I walk her to the door. “What did you learn about yourself today, Akira?”

“That I’m not as worthless as I thought?”

Akira tends to end her revelations with a question mark rather than a period. "Is that a statement or a question?" I ask.

She grins. "Statement."

"For next week, I want you to journal about what it feels like to have accomplished all these challenges."

Akira nods and heads out the door.

In two weeks, I will have a sit-down with Akira and her dad to update our goals, not the least of which is to obtain answers about where Akira stands financially. As a tutor it would be none of my business to seek those answers. As a life coach, I am committed to advocating for this young woman, even if it comes down to doing so in front of her father. Clarity is needed for a brighter future.

Christmas at the Hospital

CHRISTMAS CAN BE A lonely time for Jewish people. The only places open are Chinese restaurants and movie theaters. Perhaps you can invite your Jewish friends over to your house to enjoy the holiday festivities.

You say your house will be filled to capacity? Suggest your friend volunteer at a hospital. Every year, the Jewish Federation provides volunteers to staff local hospitals, enabling hospital personnel to spend Christmas with their families. Your friend performs a good deed and receives a free meal at the end of the shift—a win-win situation.

I encourage Akira to volunteer for our local volunteer event. "It would be a fun experience for you."

Akira shrugs. "I guess you can sign Dad and me up for something."

I pull up the available time slots on their website. From the looks of it, a majority of volunteer shifts are already full or begin at 7:00 a.m.

"A good number of these volunteer positions involve social interaction," says Akira. "Dad and I aren't comfortable talking to strangers."

"No greeter positions, then. How about delivering food to patients' rooms?"

Akira considers this possibility. "I'll be given a cart with a list of what tray goes to what room. It shouldn't be too difficult to complete. More than likely they'll have one of the staff there to assist me."

We finally zero in on two available serving slots. Akira completes the online form. "I bet this time slot is empty because people don't want to give up their dinner."

Akira texts her dad with the plan. "He seems to be on board for the idea. After all, it's not like we have anything else to do besides sit on our butts munching on Chinese take-out and watching television."

Akira complains that her dad and sister engage in fun activities together, but not with her. Volunteering will provide a great bonding experience. To his credit, Mark agrees.

Not saying *no* is a big deal for Mark. This man is more quiet and reserved than my own husband, which is saying a lot. To Mark, a highly educated engineer, sharing confidences of the heart is like being asked to lead an expedition to Pluto. Wait! Is that still even considered a planet?

My hubby cops out on volunteering, but I sign up for the 7:00 a.m. shift to deliver meals to patients' rooms. By the time I step off the elevator and onto the basement level, the kitchen volunteers are already delivering the meals. The supervisor has no clue where to put me. She tells me to wait.

It is eerily quiet in this industrial-sized kitchen. Only two staff members and me. The hands on the wall clock tick as slowly as a turtle with rheumatoid arthritis.

Thirty minutes later, a handful of kitchen staff members take their places along a conveyor belt. The supervisor instructs me to put on a pair of plastic gloves. Then she demonstrates the finer points of loading dirty plates and cups onto a conveyor belt. As I load rack after rack of dinnerware, I recall Akira's boyfriend is a dishwasher in Denmark. I've always considered this job to be menial labor.

But now, after actually engaging in these tasks, I realize dishwashing requires a cool head to quickly dump food, spray off dishes, load dishes onto endless racks, and send those racks down the assembly line conveyor belt. All the while, the commercial dishwasher rumbles in the background and water from an oversized spray drips onto the skid-free mat.

There is a rhythm to this work. An undercurrent of words, punctuated by an occasional laugh, can be heard amidst the ear-splitting roar of the dishwasher and dryer. It's all about efficiency, pacing, teamwork, and having fun.

Soon, my shift is over and it's time for me to go home. I shake hands with each worker and mention how much I enjoyed working alongside them today. They smile politely, and then resume their duties. The supervisor walks me to the elevator and mentions that kitchen and cleaning staff earn the least monetary compensation of all hospital workers—just $7.25 per hour.

As I ride the elevator upstairs to the main lobby, I acknowledge my street smarts have skyrocketed. Each of us blithely goes about our daily lives oblivious that one speck of bacteria on a dish of food being served to us can be life threatening. These workers at the bottom of the pay scale save our lives every day.

This is the lesson I need impart to Akira during our next life-coaching session: Respect all workers in our society, no matter their level of education, no matter their hourly rate or annual salary. One more idiom: Don't judge others until you've walked in their shoes.

Meeting about the Future

IT IS OUR FIRST session of the New Year. Akira and I sit cross-legged on the carpeted floor in my home office, discussing her future. She is adamant about eventually moving to the Netherlands to live with Damon, her fiancé of eight years. The young man, who also has Asperger's, has visited Akira in the United States on a few occasions. Although he holds a menial job back home, he does live in his own apartment. Mark likes him.

"Why wait to live your life?" I ask. "You can get a job there."

"My doctor says I have a fifty-percent chance of getting BRCA1," says Akira. Her hands are trembling.

I shudder. Ovarian cancer, like her mom. "All the more reason for you to move sooner than later."

"I need to get tested every six months."

"They must have excellent hospitals in the Netherlands."

"Dad wants me to stay here for the surgery."

"If the time comes, you can always fly back home."

Akira shrugs.

As in past sessions, I remind myself I am Akira's life coach, not her mommy. I switch gears. "How's the job search going?"

Akira frowns. "Not so good."

"Would you consider fast food restaurants?"

"I'm not good filling orders or handling money."

"How do you know? Have you ever tried?"

"I just know I'd get an anxiety attack," she mutters.

"What would be scary about working behind the counter?"

"Having to fulfill the customer's expectations."

Whoa. I didn't see that one coming. "Can you elaborate?"

Akira shivers. "All those people in line. I'd be scared I'd drop something or give out the wrong change."

"Then what would happen?"

"The customer would get mad and start screaming at me."

"Do you think people are basically nice or mean?"

"Basically mean," she answers without hesitation.

Whoa!

"My sister says I'm clumsy and can't do anything right," Akira continues. "She says I make a fool out of myself."

"Do you think most people are like your sister?"

She nods.

I am incredulous. "What does your dad say?"

"He agrees."

"So he's told you you're clumsy and can't do anything right?"

"No, but he always says don't make a fool of myself."

A great idea pops into my head. "Let's call your job coach from the Autism Society and ask if she's noticed any changes in you lately."

Two minutes later, Sheri, the job coach, is on loudspeaker. "Akira, you've really come a long way in how you present yourself at interviews. You're more confident than you used to be. You look an interviewer in the eye—something you never did before. And you converse with the interviewer in complete sentences, not just in monosyllables. I'm confident we're going to find you a job."

We ask Sheri if fast food is an option. Although Sheri confirms that choice, Akira says she doesn't feel comfortable going down that path. I thank Sheri and remind her to notify Akira before sending out any more resumes. Then I whisper for Akira to thank her for all her help.

Today, Akira and I log into a community college website, the same college she attended for her gaming courses. This time, we explore other courses of study she might be interested in.

"How about data entry?" I ask.

Akira shakes her head.

"Computer programming?"

Akira wrinkles her nose.

"How about computer repair? You're good at fixing things."

"Too stressful."

I throw up my hands. "So what do you want to do?"

"I really want to be a dog groomer," she confides.

"Fine." I search for an appropriate website. "There's a school right here in North Carolina."

Akira's eyes turn glassy. "I'm scared I'd cut their nails too short and make them bleed."

"How about a veterinary assistant who works behind the front desk?"

Akira's body shakes. "People bring sick dogs into PetSmart. Sometimes they've been in accidents. Really scary stuff."

"But how often does that happen? Usually you'll just be checking in the dog or cat for a doctor's appointment."

Akira shakes her head. "Not for me."

We discuss possibilities in the healthcare field. Phlebologist (Too much blood.)

CNA. (Don't like being around old people.)

Ultrasound Technician. (I might make a mistake.)

I am losing patience. "Seriously, Akira. You've got an excuse for everything. You've got to start somewhere, unless you want to wash dishes like your boyfriend."

She totally misses my drift. "I wouldn't mind doing that, but I've never gotten called for an interview."

"The bottom line is, you can't independently live on $7.75 per hour, and your dad wants you to find a job that will enable you to eventually reach that goal."

"We're checking into SSI for people with disabilities, as well."

This is a surprise. "You never mentioned that before."

"That's because we weren't sure we'd get it. We've been trying for years, but now it's looking good."

I must admit I am feeling a tang of jealousy at being left out of the loop.

"If I get SSI," she continues, "I'll only be allowed to work up to twenty hours per week."

"That's all the hours we're looking at anyway. Did you ask your dad if your mom left you money in a trust fund? You might very well have enough money to retrain for a better paying job."

"I don't have any money," Akira insists. "That's why I'm so lucky Dad is letting me stay at the house. I'm just a squatter, eating up all Dad's food, using up all his electricity."

I roll my eyes. "We've discussed this before. You are his daughter. It is your house, too."

"Annie says that since I don't pay rent and since I don't make any money, nothing here is mine. Not even the computer. Dad bought me that, too, once we decided to get the more expensive gaming version."

Before I can respond, my dogs begin yakking. Someone's at the door.

It's Mark, right on time for our family meeting.

I wave Akira's dad into a chair in my home office. "We're trying to come up with a plan to pursue or retrain for a new career."

We recount the options Akira and I discussed. "What are your thoughts?"

Mark leans back in his chair. "I definitely don't want her taking more college classes."

"You understand that at this point, Akira can only expect to get a minimum-wage job," I remind him.

"That's fine. I just want her to get started."

"How do you foresee her eventually living independently?"

"We'll cross that bridge when we come to it."

I take a deep breath. "Akira thinks she has no money and is being allowed to live in your house through your good graces."

"That's ridiculous," he scoffs.

"Did her mother leave her any money when she died?"

He nods.

"Does Akira have access to that money?"

"She'll have access to it when I die."

"The thing is, Akira needs to be able to access some of that money now so she doesn't feel destitute."

"I buy her whatever she needs."

"It's a matter of Akira believing you trust her to handle her own money."

"I don't know if she's ready to handle her own money. She would just throw her money away on computer games."

"Akira is twenty-seven years old. You say you want her to learn the skills to become independent. Have you taught her how to balance her checkbook?"

He shakes his head. "I do it for her."

Akira interrupts. "You find my checkbook, even when I hide it."

I let that statement pass. "Have you shown her how to deposit and withdraw money from the bank? Does she even know what her bank account number is?"

"I deposit money into her checking account when it runs low."

It is obvious Mark is operating on two conflicting belief systems: He wants to keep Akira financially dependent on him, and he wants her to move out and live independently. No wonder he and his daughter are both confused and frustrated.

"Mark, you need to meet with a financial planner from the bank—if you don't already have your own person—and set up an account in Akira's name so she has control over a portion of her inheritance while you are still alive."

Mark looks pensive.

"The only way you'll know if she can conscientiously handle money is by giving her an opportunity to do so. First, teach her some mini-lessons on what we just discussed, as well as how to balance her own checkbook. If you need to see her checkbook, please ask her first. We're talking respect, here. Does that sound kosher?"

Mark slaps his palms on his knees and rises to his feet. "Sounds like a plan."

On their way out the door, Akira sends me a grateful smile.

If only we parents could see how our attitude toward our children affects their feelings of self-worth.

Exhausted, I shut the front door.

Path to Adventure

AKIRA IS READY TO embark on new adventures, this I know with certainty. So far, we've successfully addressed basic grooming, cooking, baking, shopping for food and clothes, volunteering in the community, starting a pet sitting service, completing three speeches at Toastmasters, and getting her driver's license.

I wish I'd had a life coach during my growing-up years, someone to emotionally support me through the rough spots of my parents' divorce. I was only six years old at the time, way too young to be a batting board for my parents' acrimonious words toward each other. Way too young for my father to leave me.

But I have been there for my own kids, and I will continue to be there for Akira. My husband says I'm a mother figure to Akira, taking over where her mom left off. The Temple's membership director, a long-time friend of Akira's mom, says it's more than that. "You've taken her in directions her parents could not imagine. It's amazing how much Akira has changed."

Unfortunately, Akira's dad still doubts her abilities, and Annie continues to denigrate each accomplishment with a caustic remark. I wonder whether her comments stem from guilt that she has not provided the love and emotional nourishment siblings should provide to each other. Why hasn't Annie been the one to take her sister clothes shopping or to get a manicure?

How different my life might have been if I'd had a sister or brother. Together, my sibling and I would have weathered our parents' tumultuous divorce. We would have confided in each other, laughed together, become each other's best friend.

For many families, these fantasies have little connection to reality. Steel walls of resentment and jealousy build up between siblings over the years.

Akira views herself as one of my kids. Yet, it is Annie's love and acceptance she hungers for. Unfortunately, jealousy and resentment harden her sister's heart.

Each of us views life through a subjective lens weathered by years of joyful or debilitating encounters we experienced as children. Did we thrive on words of endearment or wither from verbal attack? Did we reach for hugs or shrink from beatings? Were our accomplishments applauded or ridiculed by our parents?

Once we have children, we either continue the way we were raised or carve a new beginning for ourselves and our families.

When we have children with special needs, however, those carvings become jagged scars. We are at a loss for how to proceed.

Experts are called in to intercede. Children are sent to audiologists, developmental optometrists, occupational therapists, physical therapists, speech therapists, psychologists, ADD tutors, counselors, and organizations, all in an attempt to fix the child. But there is no magic pill.

Then a tutor or life coach comes along and rocks the boat. Parents are asked to view their special needs adult child as a competent functioning individual. It is nothing short of a miracle that this mind shift occurs. But it does. It needs to for that young adult to thrive and not just exist. Expectations must be high, but not out of reach. Just high enough to be attainable.

As Akira says, "It just takes one person to remove the blinders and lead an adult child down the path to independence."

Akira Gets a Job

Akira calls to say she finally got a job. "The ticket taker position at the movie theatre?" I ask.

"The sales associate at PetSmart," she says proudly. "I get to work in the pet care section. The birds, small animals, and fish are my job, along with any supplies their owners need. This is going to be awesome."

This job was four years in the making. "Congrats!"

"It's nine hours a week," she says.

"It's a start," I say. "As time goes by and you learn the job, they'll schedule you for more hours."

"I don't know. Nine hours is a lot."

I chuckle. "You need to get used to working again, kiddo. What will your training involve?"

"I'll be shadowing other associates to learn what my job as a pet care associate entails. So far, I have read the company booklet and taken the prerequisite tests. But other than that, my knowledge of caring for small animals is somewhat lacking. I mean I haven't had a bird or hamster in over a decade."

Akira mentions the Autism Society has assigned her an on-site job coach to ensure her negative emotions don't get triggered as she learns to perform her duties.

My hackles go up. A sentry to observe every moment of Akira's work shift? The other employees will consider her a dimwit. "Is she going to be there permanently?"

"No, she'll be with me at work three times a week for two months and then slowly back off."

"Whatever you feel is best, kiddo."

"It's just until I'm ready to work solo."

"As long as it's a temporary situation, that should be okay," I say brightly. "How are you going to get there?"

"The hours are a bit crazy since I'll be going in before the store opens. Dad's going to drive me back and forth to work the first couple of days. I've never driven alone that far before."

"What is it, like twenty minutes?"

"More like twenty-five or thirty," she complains.

"You're just driving down one road the whole way. You'll be fine."

"I'm not sure," Akira worries. "What if they put me on an early morning or night shift and I have to drive alone in the dark? I'm bad at directions, and I'll get lost. I don't know if I can do it."

"We all feel unsure of ourselves when we first start driving. You'll become more confident after you do it a while. Besides, you've got your GPS."

"Maybe," she says hesitantly.

"You finally got your dream job working with pets. Enjoy it."

"How did your first couple of days on the new job go?" I ask Akira. We are meeting at my house for our weekly session.

"I shadowed a pet care associate named Rick. He's a sixty-year-old man with gray hair and a scruffy beard. He's also taller and stronger than I am. This guy carried a forty-pound bag of bird bedding to the bird habitat because my wimpy frame couldn't even get said bag a foot off the ground."

"You'll gain strength in your upper body as time goes by."

"Then Rick opened the bird cages and showed me how to remove the trays, spray them with disinfectant, and then reset the cages so they looked nice and clean. It was a lot of information to take in, so my job coach made a list for me to check off."

"Check-off lists are always a great idea."

"Then Rick showed me how to clean the hamster cages. It took ninety percent of my work shift to clean them because I had trouble dumping the dirty bedding into the garbage can without it going all over the floor. By the time I left work, my arms felt like they were going to fall off."

"Ouch," I wince empathetically.

"The next day I was greeted by two of the managers. One of them asked me what size shirt I wear so they could get me an associate's shirt.

"I tried to look at the tag on my shirt and told them I think it's a medium. I needed to wait a few days to get mine, so until then I had to wear either a red or blue t-shirt with khaki pants. No open-toed shoes either.

"Then Rick told my job coach and me to follow him to the habitat for small animals, which took up two aisles. There were eight cages on both aisles and two on the end facing the middle of the store. Rick showed me how to get the cages out to clean them. They were heavy."

"How much did each cage weigh?" I ask.

"My guess is they weighed about ten pounds, as much as Misty Dog."

"You really need to do some weight lifting, kiddo," I joke.

"I had five hours to clean all eighteen cages, many of which contained up to six hamsters each. I looked at the cages, then at Rick, and back to the cages. He just told me to clean one side today and the other side next week."

"Thank goodness."

"Rick left me to clean the cages while my job coach hovered around the area watching me. I was nervous about making a mistake with her watching. I didn't want to look like I was hired for a job I couldn't do correctly."

"She's there to help, not judge, Akira."

"I guess. It took me my entire shift to get through all the cages. At one point my job coach tried to help me sweep up bedding. One of the managers yelled at her that it was my job and she should only be watching, not helping. I agreed that I wouldn't learn anything if I was being babied for a mess I made. This was my job, so I needed to take responsibility for my messes and clean them up myself."

"You showed you are a responsible person."

"By the time I left for the day, I had several bites on my hands from pissed off animals upset with me messing with their homes. Who knew a chinchilla could break through a pair of surgical gloves?

"Rick called him a *chin-killa* and said it was a rite of passage to get bitten by him. I found myself wondering if that creature would ever get bought. He's been here since Christmas, and it's already February. Guess you can't judge a book by its cover, or in this case, a chinchilla by its teeth."

"You're a funny one," I say playfully. "Any other training?"

Akira nods. "I learned to clean fish tanks, to bag crickets, and I had to take even more tests before I was deemed ready to join the work force as a paid employee. I just hope I do a good job and make them proud."

"Great job," I say.

There's nothing like the feeling of success.

Six weeks into her new job, Akira says she was asked to go to the manager's office. "I was scared I was in trouble for something. Had I bagged the fish wrong? Was I too quiet? It turned out I was taking too long cleaning the cages.

"I also forgot to put the water and food dishes back in the bird's cages and didn't tell anyone. No one noticed until closing when one of the employees found the dishes in the sink. I bowed my head and told the manager I was very sorry and I'd do my best to work faster."

Tough love is needed here. "Dogs bow their heads, not people, unless you're praying or being sentenced in court for a crime you committed," I say harshly.

"Okay," she says meekly.

"Have you had your first evaluation yet?" I ask, my voice calmer now.

Akira nods. "When I was scolded for being forgetful, I made sure that mistake never happened again."

The punitive terminology Akira uses freaks me out. "Akira, children get scolded. You are a twenty-seven-year-old woman."

"I know," Akira says sheepishly. Then she continues. "While I was busy focusing on getting faster at cleaning the cages, another incident happened.

"I was showing a father and his two sons a hamster. It got loose and landed on the floor.

"'Runaway rodent,' I yelled. 'Quick, catch it!' I tried to corral the small animal into a plastic igloo.

"The father and his sons dropped to their hands and knees, and we each took an aisle trying to catch Speedy Gonzales before he could get hurt.

"'He's under the shelving on aisle twenty,' the dad called to me as I crawled along aisle eighteen looking for the escapee.

"With help from Jeff, another coworker, we managed to pin the hamster under aisle twenty and, using a broom, were able to get him back into the igloo and into his cage.

"I wiped dust and dirt off my pants. Then I asked them if they still wanted the escape artist or wanted to see another hamster?

"The dad shook his head and said, 'I don't think the boys are ready for a hamster just yet. Thank you though.'"

"You tell the best stories, Akira," I marvel. "So, you got a bad evaluation because you asked the customers to help grab the hamster?"

Akira shakes her head. "I got a bad evaluation because I let the hamster out of the cage without making sure he had a container to go into."

This is one of those teachable moments. "Do you think it was okay to ask the customers to help you find the hamster?"

"I called out for help, but none of the other staff members were nearby. My job coach left two weeks ago, so she couldn't help."

"Is there a loud speaker or a way to call the cashier's area?"

"I guess I could ask about that."

"Good idea."

It's eight weeks into her new job and I'm listening to a trilogy of Akira's escapades: There's the python that escaped from sickbay, the hamster who dashed into the cat room, and the customer who questioned what temperature to cook a dog at.

Not all of Akira's pet store experiences are funny; some are downright sad. Like the batch of hamsters who developed wet-tail or the hundreds of fish who died in one fell swoop when the aquarium filtration system went out.

On the whole, Akira is rising to the occasion on every level. She is building body muscle by lifting and cleaning forty- to fifty-pound cages and pouring eight hundred goldfish into an aquarium. She is building confidence by successfully handling all kinds of animals, including ferrets, tarantulas, birds, hamsters, frogs, scorpions, and reptiles.

Akira recently confided, "My sister told me I could never take care of a dog all on my own. Here I am taking care of an entire pet store."

It just goes to show we never know what a person is capable of until we give them an opportunity to shine.

Reflections

TODAY, I'M REACHING OUT to my special education teacher friend, Geri, back in Chicago. In recent months, my writing, tutoring, and life coaching has left me little time to connect with friends. Ugh! Even the way I just worded that thought makes me sound like a *victim*. If Akira had tossed me that foul ball, I would have immediately jumped on her about "no excuses."

However, I *choose* to remain incognito from my friends while I create stories and buoy my students. If I was naive enough to share this speck of not-so-thrilling truth to Geri, she'd retort, "So how's that working out for you?"

Instead of apologizing for my friend-sabbatical when Geri answers the phone, I expound on Akira's amazing strides over the last eight months. "When I first met her, she was isolated and insulated. No driver's license, afraid of venturing out into the community. Now she drives thirty minutes back and forth to work, as well as to our Toastmasters meetings. The cool thing is that now she zips along at or slightly above the speed limit, instead of driving five to ten miles per hour below the speed limit."

"Oh, no. She drives just like you!" Geri teases.

My friend's jab flies below my radar. "You should see her deliver a seven-minute speech in front of a group of ten fellow Toastmasters. She related well to the audience today. Turns out she's got a terrific sense of humor."

"That's impressive for someone with autism," says Geri. "I've read that seventy-five percent of people would prefer to die rather than give a speech in public."

I agree. "Socialization wise, I always invite Akira to join me for lunch in the building cafeteria after we finish our Toastmasters meeting. But this time, she was proactive and asked me."

"Really?"

"As we were getting into our respective cars to go home, she asked me to come to her house to work on her third speech together. Normally, she would never ask for a change in plan mid-stream."

"Sounds like you're doing a bang-up job with Akira," says Geri.

Immediately, my insecurity kicks in. "Her speech delivery today wasn't totally perfect. She raised her elbows like a chicken when she leaned on the podium, and she still shows autistic or immature behaviors, like acting out 'cucoo' with her hands when she was speaking."

"Does Toastmasters expect its members to be perfect?"

My insecurity slinks away. "Of course not."

"It's not like she's your puppet, with you controlling her every motion, right?"

"Okay, okay. I get the message."

"That's good, because we wouldn't want you to be getting a big head."

I laugh. "I know I'm not God, but did She get my text message?"

Geri chuckles. "You're funny. I so miss walking around the

neighborhood with you on the weekends."

"You need a laugh, I'm still available by phone," I say.

"But you're never available," she complains.

No way am I getting pulled into this discussion. I steer the conversation back to my life coaching student. "Akira is getting along well at PetSmart, too. Her manager wants to train her on all shifts because she's learning so fast. Akira also made friends at work, which is huge."

Unlike me, Geri is too polite to point out I've ditched the friend issue. Instead she says, "I'm so glad you are seeing positive results with Akira. Did you finally tell her and her dad she's your first life coaching student?"

Suddenly, I'm scratching my elbow like Akira does when she's nervous. "I planned to mention it early on, but after all the strides she's made, it seemed like a moot point."

Geri doesn't smoosh my nose in it. "Hey, you know what's best, and it sounds like she's doing great."

"I'm just blessed that God enabled me to lead this young woman down a positive path," I say, my voice humble.

"Baruch Ha'Shem," says Geri.

Thank you, God.

Literal Thinking

AKIRA IS COMING ALONG nicely in our coaching sessions, so after today's session, I treated her to a giant bag of popcorn at Walmart. It is nearing five p.m. as we exit the store, and the parking lot is packed, with cars coming and going. Despite the heavy traffic, Akira and I blithely make our way through the parking lot, deep in conversation.

Just ahead we see a young mother with her little girl. I stop in my tracks like a beagle who's found a squirrel. Mom pushes a filled shopping cart with one hand and holds her cell phone in the other hand. She chats into her phone while her little girl dances behind her as they head towards their car. I glance back at Akira. From her blank expression, I can tell she's noticed nothing out of the ordinary.

I approach the young mother and tap her on the shoulder. She whirls around to look at me, still holding the phone to her ear. "Cars are pulling in and out of here," I say. "You need to hold your daughter's hand so she won't get killed!"

The young mother smiles at me. Then she continues through the parking lot, still steering her shopping cart instead of her daughter.

Sighing, I turn to Akira. "What did you think of that?"

This time, there is no evidence of her usual question marks at the end of her response. "It was rude to interrupt that woman while she was talking on the phone," Akira says solemnly.

Literal thinking is, indeed, a characteristic of autism, but I am still baffled by her response. "What did you think of the little girl dancing through the busy parking lot while her mom paid her no attention?"

"The little girl liked to dance," says Akira, her tone matter-of-fact.

"If that was your daughter, would you hold her hand or let her dance around?"

Akira stops to think. "I don't know. She was having fun."

"Just to let you know," I say brusquely, "you always hold a child's hand in a parking lot, especially in such a dangerous situation as this is."

"Okay," she says.

As we get into my car, I mentally list *literal thinking* and *empathy* as areas we need to work on. Two steps forward, one step back, as they say.

Akira May Have Cancer

AKIRA AND I ARE brainstorming another Toastmasters speech when she receives a voicemail message from her doctor's nurse: "You have three cysts and your CA125 went up a few points."

We've all heard about doctors tersely telling their patients via telephone: "You have cancer." But this is the first time I've been present when that bombshell hits. "Oh my God," I cry.

Akira calms me down. "The marker only rose one or two points, so there's nothing to worry about. I'll find out the exact number when I go in for my biopsy tomorrow."

A few points is such an ambiguous term, the kind of ambiguity people with ADHD like me can't handle. "Akira," I insist, "you really need to get your facts straight. Let's go online to check what the baseline should be."

We go online and discover the normal baseline is thirty-five, anything above is a red flag. Normally Akira's number is in the mid-twenties range.

Akira's cell phone rings a second later. It's the technician who performed her ultrasound. Akira puts the call on speaker mode so I can hear.

Together, we have compiled a list of four questions, but Akira feels nervous posing these questions herself. In the past, her mom or dad had interceded on her behalf. For Akira, this stepping-up-to-the-plate is new and scary; she must rely on herself instead of her parents to gain her personal medical information.

Akira timidly speaks into the phone. "What was my normal CA125, and how many points has it gone up?"

The technician responds. "Your first two CA125s were twenty-six and twenty-seven. This one is fifty-nine."

Akira looks as shocked as I feel. "It more than doubled in the last six months," she whispered to me.

The technician continues. "You have three cysts on your ovaries, none of which appear cancerous. Endometriosis or fibroids may have caused the increase. We'll do another ultrasound next month just to be certain."

When Akira gets off the phone, I say, "They can't be too worried if they're scheduling your ultrasound test a month out."

"I hope not," Akira says, her eyes teary.

A second later her phone rings again. This time it's Mark. Akira had given him prior permission to receive her medical information. "Get yourself over to the doctor's office. They're doing your vaginal ultrasound today."

Akira clicks off the phone. "I don't know how he managed to do it."

Akira is relieved when the nurse tells her she can do the less painful epidermal version if she downs three bottles of water before the test.

"Want me to drive you to the hospital?" I ask.

Akira sighs in relief. "Please? Normally I don't jump at the chance to have someone act as my wingman, but right now, you're the only female role model within driving distance from me. I need you there in case I freak out."

"Hey, I'm your life coach. I'm going to be right by your side."

We leave for the hospital as Akira chugs bottle after bottle of water.

At the doctor's office, we wait for the nurse to call Akira's name. Meanwhile, she updates me on her cancer testing history. "A while ago I took a blood test to learn more about my family genetics involving cancer. I lost my maternal grandmother to breast cancer and my mother to ovarian cancer. Both grandparents on my dad's side had a form of cancer. Sadly, my blood test came back positive for BRCA1, which means I have a higher risk for ovarian, colon, and breast cancer. I have enlarged lymph nodes under my left arm and some cysts in my breasts, so I need to get a biopsy done to be certain they're not cancerous.

"When Dad told me about the phone call, I had an anxiety attack and hid in my room to be alone. My tears rushed out like Niagara Falls. I was not prepared for something like being diagnosed with BRCA1."

"Are there precautions you have to take?" I ask.

"I need to get CA125 tests, mammograms, and ultrasounds on a regular basis."

High blood pressure, not cancer, runs in my family, so I'm clueless about the terms she is using. "What's a CA125 test?"

"It's a blood test that looks for elevated levels of a certain antigen."

"How did your dad react when he found out your blood test came back positive?"

"He's a strong guy, so seeing him cry just showed how much the news hurt."

Just then, the nurse calls Akira's name. I hang out in the waiting room, journaling while Akira does her thing. I reflect on how the description of a life coach constantly fluctuates, according to what a client needs in a given moment. In one year, I've graduated from basic grooming instructor to guardian angel, as Akira calls me.

The test takes an hour and a half because even though Akira has consumed sixty-four ounces of water, the nurse is unable to get an exact scan.

Upon receiving Akira's diagnostic results, her doctor conveys the results. "None of the cysts appear cancerous, we'll leave them alone."

"We scheduled a meeting with Dr. Clark Pearson and his nurse, Lyn," Akira tells me. "He's the doctor who oversaw Mom's chemotherapy, hysterectomy, and overall cancer treatment from start to finish."

"It sounds like you're comfortable with that medical team."

Akira nods. "Lyn was always so happy to see me when I came with Mom to her chemo treatments, even if I did fall asleep in the chair on several occasions. Their examining room is cold and the cold makes me sleepy. Plus, it always took several hours to complete that day's chemo.

"I'm curious what their plan will be for me. All we know is I have BRCA1, my CA125 is doubled, and I have cysts on my ovaries. I already know I need to get surgery within the next two years."

Life-altering Surgery

It is eight days before Akira's surgery, and she's in a mind-spin. "I will be losing both my ovaries and put on hormone therapy for the rest of my life."

"Why two? I thought only one ovary was cancerous."

"I don't want to go through two surgeries with no idea when the second one will happen. I don't need the added stress."

So sad.

"I just turned twenty-eight and already I'm having to make a drastic decision about my future health, but both my doctors agree that my logic behind this radical idea is sound," she says.

"What about having kids?"

"Damon and I decided not to pass that autistic gene down. We're not going to have kids. Plus, I can hardly take care of myself. How would I take care of a kid?"

Probably a good decision.

Akira mentions she posted on Facebook, informing her friends and family of the news.

"Can I see?" I ask.

She pulls it up for me on her phone:

> I'm not usually one to drop bad news on people but unfortunately this needs to be said. I have something called BRCA1. This is a gene mutation that is associated with a higher risk of breast and ovarian cancer.
>
> A few months ago, one of my ultrasounds came back with some bad news: I have three cysts on my ovaries; two normal and one compound. While I have been told that these will not become cancerous, the only way to remove them safely is to have surgery to remove my ovaries.
>
> This will happen on August 2nd. I have been told that the recovery time is six weeks. Please keep me in your prayers and here's hoping the surgery goes well.

"You were fearless to put yourself out there like that," I muse.

"I was amazed how many people responded! My Aunt Marley, who was one of the first five people to respond, told me I was brave for going through this. By the next day three people had left emoji's and six people had replied. The Temple director told me the whole Temple is praying for me."

"How did all these supportive responses make you feel?"

"It's nice to know there are people out there who care enough to respond. I honestly never expected to get this much response for a Facebook post. Not one comment was insulting and their comments made me happy to know that people out there, even if we haven't talked in years, still care about me."

Too bad it takes a wedding, surgery, or funeral for people to recognize how special their loved ones are, I muse. Heaven on earth will occur when families and friends made us feel valued and cared for every day of the year.

August second, the day of the surgery. I phone to wish Akira good luck.

"Hello?" she says groggily.

I check the time. Seven a.m. "Aren't you supposed to leave your house at eight o'clock?"

"I'm getting up now."

The birds are singing, the sun is out, and Akira almost missed the most important appointment of her life. "How long does it take you to get to the hospital?"

"It takes an hour and a half. Before Dad and I leave, I need to shower with the bottle of surgical soap they gave me."

She's scheduled for 10:00. Once again, I remind myself I am not her mom. "Then I'll let you get to it. Good luck."

I text Akira later that afternoon. "How did the surgery go?"

"Dad and I arrived at the hospital just in time to check in. We went to admissions and pulled a number. A while later we found out we were in the wrong area and were shown where to go.

"I was given an armband twice the size of my wrist—I have tiny wrists, a trait mom and I shared.

"Three hours later I was called to the back and had to give blood, personal information, and answer some questions. The doctor marked my stomach with black marker where they would need to operate. The felt tip tickled a little.

"I changed into a hospital gown and met the medical team. They put an IV in my right arm and a saline drip IV in my left. Then they gave me what Annie calls happy drugs because they make you feel woozy and silly.

"Before the medicine fully kicked in, I learned that years ago, when Dad had been waking up from anesthesia after his colonoscopy, he'd proposed to his nurse. He tried to explain it to me as they wheeled my hospital bed into the surgery room. I couldn't help giggling. The last thing I remember before going to sleep was six people in the room telling me to breathe into the face mask, a massive light fixture over my head, and the beeping of a machine taking my vitals."

"And the surgery itself?" I ask.

"When I came to, I learned the surgery was a success, but there had been a minor issue where one of my ovaries had been dangerously close to my colon," said Akira. "They managed to remove both with little issue. I could only groggily moan and groan. I was far too out of it to respond with words."

"Great news. And how are you feeling now?"

"I'm okay. It took an hour before my vision returned and I could talk. I can feel the loss of the mass. On top of that, I have five incisions in my lower stomach, one in my belly button and two on either side. They gave me three different painkillers, two stool softeners, and my hormone replacement medicine."

"Now all you need is some R and R," I say.

"I guess."

I spent the next few days taking care of one of my dogs experiencing gastrointestinal problems. Finally, Rocky and I dropped by Akira's house for a visit. I brought homemade matzo ball soup, although it is weird cooking it in the heat of August. Akira lapped that soup up like a puppy.

"Haven't you been eating?"

"No appetite."

"So you've just been resting since you got home?"

Akira nods. "Also walking around the house three times a day, like the nurse said to do. My stitches itch, though."

"How have you been managing since you got home?"

"I went home in the pouring rain and had to use the walker to get to Dad's bed on the first floor. I didn't have the strength to go up the stairs. This must have been a flashback moment for Dad because it was the same place Mom had to recover previously."

"Your dad had no problem sleeping upstairs?"

"He originally wanted me to spend my recovery on the living room couch. I told him this was a bad idea because I could easily fall off. It also smells like Misty and sweaty Dad!

"On top of that, he didn't want me to use the walker. He thought my balance would be fine and that I would be on my feet within a day or two. It was probably hard to picture his young daughter needing to use the walker for balance. I finally convinced him that sleeping in his first-floor bedroom and using the walker for the first week or two would be necessary until I felt stronger."

Several days later, Akira phones me. "I've been back in the hospital."

Shit. "Why?"

"I was dry heaving into a red plastic basin. This went on for three hours, every fifteen minutes. I would try to sleep only to wake up a short while later and vomit. It got to the point I was barfing stomach acid, which only made it worse.

"Dad called Lyn, my nurse. She told me to wait it out.

"Two hours later she called back to say I should come in. They wanted to be certain I hadn't gotten an infection and make sure nothing had happened during surgery. Since I was badly dehydrated, it took several attempts to fit me with an IV because the nurse couldn't find my vein.

"Once they had the IV in place, they put me in a hospital room and designated me as NFBM meaning no food by mouth. They made me drink 800 milliliters of something called contrast. It was supposed to make my organs easier to see on the CT scan.

"The fluid hadn't reached the designated point yet so I was moved back to the room. Several hours passed and it was now the middle of the night before we attempted again. The fluid had moved but still wasn't near the designated point so I was yet again sent back to my hospital room.

"They decided really early in the morning to give it one last shot. It was either I get fitted with a tube and have contrast flushed to the location or get woken up several more times. I opted for the tube, even though I knew it would hurt like crazy.

"This time the test was a success and they got a clear reading. By this time, I was sore. They gave me some new painkillers and I went to sleep. I just wanted the pain to go away. It made it hard to sleep, walk, or even get up to use the bathroom.

"I was malnourished from not eating. I was only able to eat a few bites of oatmeal and some soup. I slowly worked my way toward eating solid foods. I used the walker for a few days until my balance returned. I honestly thought I would be so high off the painkillers, I would be unable to do anything for a long time, but it didn't take as long as I thought.

"I've now moved back upstairs to my bedroom and have begun walking without the walker. So far, I've managed to take two showers without soaking the surgical tape too much. I even regained most of my appetite and weaned myself off the painkillers. I still need the occasional Tylenol or Ibuprofen, and my hormone replacement."

"Wow," I say. "You've really gone through a lot."

Akira says, "Three more weeks and I can go back to work."

First Jury Duty

Serving on a jury is one of the duties and privileges of living in a democracy. Some U.S. citizens may disagree with my word choice, due to the negative impact jury duty has on their work or childcare schedule, as well as a loss of wages. But without each of us standing up to take our turn, there would be no "jury of our peers."

That's why I was so impressed when only four weeks out of surgery, Akira answered the call to sit on a DUI case. I'd only spoken to her sporadically during her recuperation, so this was headline news. By the time we resumed our coaching sessions, she'd already completed her first jury duty.

"Why didn't you mention it to me?" I ask, perplexed.

"I didn't think it involved life coaching."

True enough. Akira is a client and not obligated to notify me of anything other than her plans to miss a lesson. "How did you feel when you got called?"

"It was my first time, so I had no idea what to expect or what to do. Mom and Dad had been called in before, but never me.

"I was really nervous the night before and didn't get much sleep. I fretted over being picked for a case. I also worried about what type of case I would be chosen for. Would it be a civil, criminal, DUI, or a personal injury case? Making decisions that affect the outcome of someone's life scares me."

"That's scary for anybody," I say.

"I'm normally a non-judgmental person and try my hardest to hear both sides of a story," she continues. "But, when put on the spot, I get nervous and second guess myself."

Heck, so would I. "What was it like when you first got to the courthouse?"

"Dad dropped me off there. The map on the summons wasn't clear. We found the parking lot perfectly fine, but we went to the wrong building. We probably looked like we were trying to break into the old courthouse. Good thing we didn't get arrested.

"Mom always told me to ask a uniformed officer for help if I was lost. I saw a police officer walk by and asked him where I was supposed to go for a jury summons. He was surprisingly nice and pointed us to the building to the left of where we were standing."

"Why do you say 'surprisingly nice'?" I ask quizzically.

"This was far different from the police officers I knew from Massachusetts, who were rude and let power go to their heads."

"You can't generalize. In every profession, you're going to get the good people as well as the power seekers."

"I guess," she says.

By now, I know that's Akira's passive way of saying, "Butt out."

"It turned out I was about an hour early. I sat outside the building with a couple other people who were also waiting to enter. The entire time I waited, I had the Pokémon Go app running and was spinning the nearby PokéStop every five minutes."

"Talk about being productive during the wait," I marvel.

Akira grins. "I'm not sure how many people would consider playing Pokémon Go to be a productive use of time.

"Finally, the doors to the courthouse opened and we were allowed inside. We put our personal belongings into brown bins and sent them through a security checkpoint. It was the same as going through the security checkpoints at the airport. I half expected them to make me take my shoes off.

"I sent my purse and phone through the scanner and walked through the checkpoint. There was a loud beeping sound. Why'd it go off? The only metal I had on me was my glasses, the metal clasp on my slacks, and a titanium wire insert in one of my lymph nodes from a biopsy months prior. None of which should have triggered the alarm."

"How did you react when you heard the beeping noise?"

"Strangely enough, I didn't have a panic attack. A female security guard had me step to the side and hold out my arms as she ran a metal detector over me. The buzzer didn't go off this time. She let me go and I picked up my bin, grabbed my things, and headed for the elevator.

"There were several other people in the elevator. Some of us headed for the third floor while others headed to the fourth. I followed the group that got off on the third floor.

"We all walked into a huge room with a large amount of very uncomfortable chairs and two big-screen TVs. A woman greeted us and scanned our summons. Once that was done, she showed us an informational video about being a juror and the different kinds of court systems.

"We had until nine o'clock before we would be called. I walked into the jury lounge area and poured myself a cup of coffee. Even after I dumped a ton of creamer and sugar in, it still tasted like watery coffee grinds. They had to be crazy if they expected us to be awake on this pathetic excuse for coffee."

An herbal tea drinker, myself, I pretend empathy.

"Nine o'clock rolled around and the woman returned. She called out thirty names for people who would be on a jury. I dreaded my name being called because I had no idea what to expect.

'Akeerooh Stone?' she asked looking around.

"'It's pronounced Ah-kear-uh. I'm used to people butchering my first name.' I walked over and joined the twenty-eight other people in the hallway.

"We all walked into the jury room and waited to see which of us would be selected. I noticed the judge looked kind of like Patrick Dempsey but with a beard. Chuckling to myself, I turned my attention to the people at the two tables. The defense and prosecutor asked everyone questions and slowly weeded down the number. Along the way my name was called.

"'Please tell us your name and what you do for a living,' the judge asked me.

'My name is Akira Stone. I currently work in a pet store.'

'Do you live with another adult, and if so, what do they do?'

'I live with my dad who works as a mechanical engineer.'

'Have you ever served on a jury before?'

'No.'

'Have you or anyone you know been part of a crime?'

"I gulped and looked at the defense attorney. 'Yes. About fifteen years ago, I was in a car accident with a friend and her grandfather. We were driving home from the synagogue when a drunk driver rammed into us. Our car was sent through a retaining wall. My friend's grandfather suffered broken ribs, and I got glass stuck in the underside of my chin. They found an open bottle of Jack Daniel's in the other car.'

"The judge then passed the questions off to the defense attorney.

'Ms. Stone, do you drink on occasion?'

'Yes, but only during the High Holidays and even then it's only a shot-glass worth.'

'You said you were in a car accident involving a drunk driver? Would you hold your experience against my client?' the defense attorney asked.

"The attorney looked to be in his fifties, with a balding head and dark gray suit. A pair of black frame glasses sat on his nose as he looked at me. 'No, I would not. These are two completely different cases.'

"They went through a few more questions with other possible jurors before thirteen were selected. I ended up making the cut, which shocked me. I was certain I'd be dismissed for the car accident and the fact I was one of the youngest ones there. What had I said that made them pick me? I know nothing about alcohol—or drinking for that matter.

"The bailiff took us to the juror's room and handed us badges. It was how we would get in and out of the building. We were then given a break for lunch, so the thirteen of us left to get food."

"Did you eat with any of the other jurors?" I ask.

Akira shakes her head. "I chatted with two of the women on the jury about restaurants nearby since we only had an hour to grab our food, eat, and return."

I recall that, twenty years ago, I'd sat on a jury for a civil case. *Why am I only remembering now, when food is mentioned?* I wonder.

"I ended up running to Jimmy John's to get a turkey sandwich. Along the way I hit a few more PokéStops. Luckily, I got back to the courthouse with time to spare. I got to bypass the security checkpoint because of the juror badge. I ate my food in the jury room and waited the remaining time."

"How did it go once the trial resumed?"

"We listened to the defense's witness, who was the man's doctor, as he explained the definition of diabetes and the differences between hyper and hypoglycemia."

"What is the difference?"

"Confusion, heart palpitations, shakiness, and anxiety are symptoms of hypoglycemia. But increased thirst, headaches, trouble concentrating, frequent peeing, blurred vision, and fatigue are symptoms of hyperglycemia. The doctor explained the defendant had been diagnosed sixteen years ago with hypoglycemia.

"Next we listened to the sheriff's side of the event. A lot of things didn't add up after what the doctor said. I still didn't understand how hypoglycemia related to the symptoms seen during the DUI arrest.

"The day ended with us watching part of the dashboard recording. The police vehicle has a camera that shows a two-hundred-and-ten-degree angle of whatever is in front of it. The defendant refused to do the one-legged stand and the breathalyzer test. He also seemed to be swaying and repeated himself a lot. I noticed the repeated phrases of 'What do you want me to do?' and 'There it is.'

"I didn't notice the swaying because the DUI had occurred at two in the morning, it was still dark outside, and the camera lens was fuzzy from the rain. All of us jurors left at five p.m. and would reconvene at nine forty-five the next day.

"When Dad picked me up, I had to stop him twice from asking me about the case since we were told not to converse about it with people outside of the jury until the trial was over."

I'm fascinated with Akira's storytelling ability, a rare trait in a person with Asperger's. Perhaps we can sign her up for the local storytelling club. "So what happened on the second day of the trial?"

"Dad and I drove back to the courthouse. I got there half an hour early and waited for them to let us in again. It was pretty hot out so I made sure to sit in the shade.

"Finally, they let us in, and I slid my juror's badge through the scanner. It let me bypass the security checkpoint again. I took the elevator with four other people.

"I was one of the first ones to arrive at the courtroom and greeted the bailiff as I walked into the juror's room. Not long afterward, the other jurors arrived. We waited for the trial to start and refreshed each other on the previous day's information to make sure we were all on the same page.

"The trial started a bit late. We joked because we were on lawyer time and walked in. Luckily, I remembered what seat I was in the day before.

"The defendant came up and gave his side of the story. His answers did not match some of the evidence we had been given. He had told the sheriff the last thing he ate was corn dogs. Yet when he retold how his day went, he told us the last thing he had eaten was grilled chicken and rice for dinner around eight p.m. and didn't have anything after. Was his loss of memory from being drunk or from having a hypoglycemic episode?

"Next, the sheriff who had made the arrest came up and answered some questions. He sounded knowledgeable about these kinds of arrests.

"With all the evidence given to us and all the witnesses put on the stand, we headed into the juror's room to figure out what to do next. We picked a foreman out of the group. Glad it wasn't me.

"From there we went over everything that had been told to us. We had people in the medical field as well as someone with diabetes on the jury. There was a lot of discussion on the symptoms of diabetes and how it was different for everyone."

"If you're diabetic, don't you have to watch your intake of carbohydrates?" I ask.

Akira nods. "The other jurors agreed that something really didn't add up here."

"How many carbs are in a can of Bud Lite?" I ask curiously.

"The man next to me pulled out his phone and checked. It was .9 grams per ounce of Bud Lite. So for a twelve ounce can that was 12 grams. We checked and found that a slice of bread had 15 grams of carbs in it. The two numbers were fairly close so we used it as a basis.

"By that logic, the man had had four slices of bread. We all agreed, with that many carbs plus his grilled chicken and rice dinner, and possibly corn dogs, there was no way he could have been hypoglycemic. If anything, he would have been *hyper*glycemic."

Exactly as I'd guessed!

Akira continued. "My fellow jurors and I went over what the doctor had said about the symptoms along with the video. He didn't show any signs of being hypoglycemic. We all agreed the doctor had only given us more information to use against him by taking the stand. It was unanimous verdict. Guilty as charged.

"The man received fifty hours of community service as well as got his license put on suspension for a period of time. All of us then left the courtroom and I called my dad to go home."

"Your suggestion that your fellow jurors compare the amount of carbs in a slice of bread to one can of beer, regarding hypo or hyperglycemia was brilliant!" I marveled.

"Dad was impressed, too, since that was one of the deciding factors. He said that was something not many people would think to ask."

"True enough."

"I only knew to ask because my mom was a dietician," says Akira. "She was always checking out carbs. Maybe Mom was looking out for me from Heaven."

"The fact is you worked as a team to problem-solve a solution. That was huge."

"I guess?"

"You need to start giving yourself credit for the good things you do, not just the mistakes you make," I tell her.

"I'm not used to getting credit for anything."

"For now, I just want you to close your eyes, take three deep breaths, and go inside yourself," I say softly. "Feel the pride of accomplishment."

After a few minutes, Akira opens her eyes. "I'm not sure if that worked, but I do feel more relaxed."

"It's a darn good start."

Yes. A darn good start.

I'm Human Like Everyone Else

Tonight, I drag Akira to an open mic at the local independent bookstore. We plan for her to read from a Toastmaster's speech she wrote on what it's like to grow up with Asperger's.

The couch in the rear of the store is comfy. Books, with subjects ranging from history to self-help, are piled on an adjacent back table. I glimpse the titles of my three published mysteries fraternizing with their neighbors on one of the eight floor-to-ceiling bookcases that frame the room.

Akira nervously picks at her face as she peruses the audience of six. The moderator tells me three other readers besides us are scheduled for this evening.

"Deep breaths, Akira, deep breaths," I whisper.

She closes her eyes and does as I ask.

I signal the moderator to allow the other three readers to go first with the hope that Akira will become accustomed to the process. As each reader steps away from the podium, I watch Akira's body relax. "Nobody's laughing at them or saying cruel things," she says, her voice incredulous.

The moderator turns in our direction. "Akira Stone will now read from 'I'm Human Like Everyone Else.' Akira?"

"Remember," I whisper, "you're teaching people what it's like to be autistic."

Akira clutches her two-page typed speech as she advances to the podium. She looks out at the small audience and hesitantly opens her lips to speak:

For years, I've felt like I've been under my dad's and other people's thumbs. Since I was little, I have always second-guessed myself. It all started when I was ten years old, after I was diagnosed with autism. At that point, my whole life went from being Akira, the goofy kid, to Akira, the girl with autism.

This diagnosis caused me to look at myself as retarded. During my elementary and middle school years, my pediatrician must have put me on half a dozen different medications. No sooner had I been put on one anti-depressant/anti-anxiety/ ADHD pill, he weaned me onto another. Some were such a high dosage for a preteen that I would regularly fall asleep in class.

An older woman sadly shakes her head in empathy with Akira.

During the next six years, I slowly began withdrawing from society. By the time I was sixteen, I had become a shut-in. I only went to school, trudged onto the bus, and came home. Occasionally, I would go to Dunkin' Donuts with some schoolmates, but we never talked. We just walked there, got our food, and rushed back to catch the bus home.

I had my first anxiety attack in the summer between eighth grade and my freshman year of high school. My Grandma Annette had died earlier that year from breast cancer, and I was depressed. If you've never had an anxiety attack, you have no idea what kind of emotional and physical pain a person goes through. In some cases, it gets to the point that not even Xanax can help. I start to shake, sweat like crazy, belch, or dry heave.

Mom and Dad took Annie and me to Disney World to get our minds off of the recent passing of Grandma. I was perfectly fine up until we got to the Logan Airport in Boston.

By the time we reached the long walkway to the elevators, I began dry heaving into a potted plant. Annie said, "Stop faking it!" while Mom rubbed my back to calm me down. I was able to regain my bearings long enough to make it through the terminal and onto the plane.

I spent the entire flight sipping a coke and trying to relax. Lo and behold, the minute we took off, Annie had her own anxiety attack. Of course, hers was the only authentic one, according to her.

The audience snickers.

We arrived at the hotel after several hours and checked in. I was feeling better by this time because we had picked a themed hotel near the Animal Kingdom. There were wild beasts outside the hotel, and I don't mean the people at the pool!

A few titters can be heard throughout the room.

Annie and I spent most of the first day wandering around the hotel. We saw everything from pelicans by the pool to water buffalo near the workout room. There were even aboriginal works of art in various places inside the hotel. Masks, weapons in display cases, and more beads than a preteen could count.

I went off by myself, wandering around, marking off the sightseeing list of animals. You got a banana split if you found all the animals. Took me a day to finish the checklist.

Someone in the audience mutters, "Yum."

During the trip, we went to Epcot to see the world stage. I unfortunately left a part of myself in every country; I dry heaved every few minutes and had to stop a lot. Annie wasn't happy with this. Add in that it was hot enough to cook an egg on the dragon statues in China!

I stayed as long as I could before the heat and my dry heaving resulted in me having to go back to the hotel. I think Mom was the one who went back with me that day. The rest of the day was too hot for Mom or me to trek around the hotel or even leave the sanctity of our air-conditioned room.

Despite my protesting stomach, the next few days were spent going to the other resorts. Animal Kingdom was my favorite, even though I got sick on one of the rides. We went on the river safari ride and part way through I got nauseous. Sensory overload.

"Poor kid," another reader blurts.

I curled up into a ball and shook like a leaf. When we finally got off the ride, I dry heaved into a trashcan. Needless to say, we didn't stay much longer. However, we did leave with a disposable camera full of pictures, a coffee mug, a beaded necklace, a handful of resort pins, four rain ponchos, and a safari hat. Not a bad haul, if I do say so myself.

Since then I've had many more episodes, and every time, they've been viewed as fake by my sister. I've told Jennie about all the occasions it has happened. She thinks I physically put myself in these situations.

I honestly don't blame her for thinking this because it's hard to break old habits. Since I have been told for years I can't do something or go somewhere without Dad or a trusted supervisor, I have gotten to the point where unless they come with me I won't leave the house.

This is what it feels like to be autistic.

The moderator raises her hands, signaling Akira's time is up. Akira exits the podium to the sound of applause. Later, the moderator congratulates her on being courageous enough to share her story, and a few members of the audience came up to share encouraging words.

I am grateful that Akira has heard these words of praise from people other than me. "You rock, kiddo! You got up there, despite your fear, and made it happen. Mazel Tov!"

Akira shrugs. "Only my dad and sister know the real me."

"Tonight, you allowed these people to see the *real you*, unclouded by the past. This is who Akira Stone is now.'"

"I guess," she says dubiously as we plop into my car.

Damaged self-esteem doesn't magically improve with revelation. It will take time.

A Disturbing Session

TODAY, AKIRA LOOKS ME in the eyes and says she feels secure and safe allowing her dad to make all her decisions. It all started a few nights ago, when I invited her to attend my book signing of *Fatal Reaction*, my third mystery.

Evidently, I'd not been specific enough for Akira when I texted her to "meet me here and we'll go together." I was referring to meeting my husband and I at my home office and I'd drive. I knew my client would feel uncomfortable driving downtown on her own.

Akira thought I meant for her to meet us at the bookstore and neglected to ask for confirmation. By the time she did ask, I was already stepping out the door.

"Meet me at the bookstore," I texted. "It will still be light outside by the time the book signing is over. You can easily follow your GPS to the store and back home."

She texted back: "Dad doesn't trust me to drive at night."

I sighed, then texted back. "No problem. Have a good night."

I arrived at the bookstore fifteen minutes early to set up my books and poster and was tickled to see my name on an outside blackboard. Catching sight of my posters in the store window and my name on the giant window calendar erased all disappointments of my day.

Imagine my pleasant surprise when five minutes before show

time, both Akira and her dad took their seats, along with several other audience members.

Later, I hugged Akira and praised her for convincing her dad to bring her. "Your presence made my book signing extra special!"

She grinned.

Next coaching session, I ask Akira why she fears driving downtown alone.

She picks at her cheeks. "I always think worst case scenario—getting lost, getting mugged."

"Lots of people feel the same way," I say. "Downtown is a big place."

"Yeah, well, I am also afraid of making a fool of myself in front of others if I get an anxiety attack."

"How so?"

"If I feel unsafe in a situation, I start belching, then dry-heaving. I need a supervisor who knows my triggers and can get me out of there before I start making a fool of myself."

So this is the reason she doesn't go anywhere by herself, aside from work and Toastmasters. "How about you supervising yourself?"

Akira vehemently shakes her head. "If I got lost, I'd just freeze. My mind would go blank. I'd go sit on the street curb, my head in my hands. I wouldn't know what to do."

Then I shared my own anxiety scenarios: interviewing for teaching jobs after being absent from the profession for several years; panicking when my husband, without so much as a heads up, brought his widowed mother to live with us. "But I got through it," I tell Akira. "A psychologist and a rabbi helped me through those times. It's hard to speak up when you feel so bad inside, but

I did, just like you are doing now."

Akira looks at me doubtfully.

We then explore all the tools she has at her disposal when she is feeling frozen. "You've been to my meditation group, so now you've got that technique down."

She nods.

"If you get lost, you can use your GPS, even if you're walking," I remind her.

"I forgot about that."

"What can you do if you begin to feel sensory overload?" I ask.

"I could try to calm myself down with the deep breathing."

"Do you think you could ask a store clerk, a customer, or a passerby for help if you were feeling dizzy or sick?"

"Um, maybe?"

My mother raised me to believe a stranger was just a friend we hadn't yet met. That's easy to do with friendly folks in Chicago and now in North Carolina. But Akira was raised to be wary of others. Even though her mother, a native Southerner, had been a nurse, her accent had been a turn-off to Northerners. (I'm embarrassed to admit I would have reacted in similar stereotype had we just met, thanks to vintage television shows, like *Beverly Hillbillies* and *Green Acres*.)

Asking Akira to reach out to strangers is like asking a rabbit to befriend a fox. But she needs to examine her stereotype, just as I did mine. Maybe she'll discover the fox is just another rabbit dressed in Halloween costume.

"No hurry. We'll take it slow, one mini-step at a time."

"I don't know if I've got the strength."

"You do, kiddo. You do."

Oil and Water

THIS WEEK I ASKED Akira to do some journaling about her relationship with her sister. I told her she could share it with me or not. She nodded as she opened the "girl talking on telephone" diary I'd given her when we first began working together. To date, my writing topics have been answered with a scarcity of thoughts and feelings, but today, I sense, will be different because of the topic: How did you and your sister get along growing up?

> *To make Annie and I get along is like trying to get oil and water to mix. It just doesn't happen. We're related by blood but not even that is enough to form a sibling relationship between us. I think it's partially my fault for not being the sister she wanted.*

> *Looking back at pictures of when I was in preschool and some of elementary school, too, it's hard to believe there are ones in which we were smiling at the camera. My favorite is of the two of us wrapped in blankets with those cardboard crowns they give out at Burger King.*

> *We were pretending we were the king and queen of some foreign country. The country was named something so silly I can't even remember what it was anymore. Mom thought we looked adorable and had us stand in the living room to take our picture. Annie still had crossed eyes back*

then and I always blinked when the shutter went off.

As years passed and the diagnosis of autism was placed on me, the two of us began having a falling out. Annie became interested in typical girl activities while I became more obsessed with video games and Japanese cartoons.

Sibling bonding? Don't make me laugh. The two of us had to be repeatedly reprimanded by Mom on many occasions. Although Annie never physically injured me, her verbal insults stampeded through my life. I always thought the lock on Annie's door when we were toddlers was to keep me from hurting her, but Dad actually said the lock was to protect me from her.

Annie got to the point where everything I did or said was wrong. I could be chewing too loudly or accidentally talk with a tiny bit of food in my mouth. No matter what it was, she'd find some way to make my life a living hell. Many of her friends would tell her of things I did, and she'd have a temper tantrum because her sister wasn't normal like her friend's siblings.

They say to learn more about a person you gotta take a walk in their shoes. Annie never even attempted to get to know me. As far as she knew, I did things to put attention on me, even if it was negative attention.

I interrupt her recitation again. "That's how all of us are, Akira. If we don't feel secure in our family's love, we either shut down or act out."

Akira looks at me pensively. "I did this because I was your average goofball of a kid?"

"Possibly."

"Some of my actions were stupid, though. I wonder if I could have done things differently. Maybe I could have bonded with Annie, doing something she liked."

"You shouldn't have been the only one doing all the trying."

Akira shrugs. "Too late now. She insults me to the point that I hide in my room."

"When are the times Annie has showed you love and attention?"

"She only came to my side to hug me and tell me everything would be all right twice in my life. The first was when we found out I was positive for BRCA1. Annie came into my room as I was bawling my eyes out and gave me a hug. She even offered to get me some kind of comfort food.

"The second time was when we found out I was getting both my ovaries removed. I felt like everything was going downhill for me. Annie again tried to cheer me up. This time she asked if I wanted any baked goods because she wanted to make me something."

I am shocked. "You have to be at death's door before your sister shows kindness?"

"It doesn't matter if I achieve something amazing, Annie won't show that kind of sisterly emotion. Not surprising, since I wasn't really that excited when she graduated with honors or got into grad school. To me it felt like she was trying to impress our parents."

"You really need to discuss this stuff with a therapist, kiddo," I advise.

Akira shakes her head. "Dad doesn't want me to share negative things about the family with anybody else."

I want to better understand where Akira is coming from, so I signal for her to continue reading:

Annie always claimed I got a lot of attention from Mom and Dad because I was autistic. I told her flat out that the attention she claimed I had gotten as a teenager was not the attention she would have been keen on gaining. "They were trying to get my mental age closer to my chronological age. You think I wanted to go through all those pragmatics classes to learn interactions that came easy to you?" I yelled at her.

"Yes, and you still got more time with Mom than I did," Annie responded without even blinking.

"Seriously, Annie? If I could go back in time and change this diagnosis so that you could be the spotlight child like you always wanted, I would. I've gotten more pain, both physical and mental, out of this diagnosis than you could possibly imagine."

You can fix crossed eyes but you can't fix autism. It doesn't work that way. Sometimes I wonder how our relationship would have been had I been diagnosed as ADHD and not autistic. It likely would have prevented a lot of our arguments and bickering.

"How do you feel after getting all those thoughts down on paper?" I ask.

Akira smiles. "Actually a lot calmer."

Revelation

Today we're going to explore more about your relationship with your sister. Are you okay with that? If not, we can work on something else."

"I'm okay with it," says Akira, but her trembling body suggests otherwise.

We do some deep breathing exercises. Then we begin. My master's degree is in special education, not counseling. However, God has given me the ability to connect on a deep level with my students and clients. Whether or not Akira realizes it, new insights and change are on her horizon.

"You previously mentioned that, besides your parents, Annie is the only person who knows the real you. Can you elaborate?"

"Nobody but my family knows that when I was a toddler, I used to punch Annie. She was only a baby."

Akira has shared this *fact* on numerous occasions, but only now does it occur to me to question that core belief. "Was your mom loving and attentive to you and your sister when you were growing up?"

"Yes."

"Do you think your mother would have stood by and allowed you to repeatedly hurt your baby sister?"

"I don't know," Akira says without a moment's hesitation.

How disconcerting. "Were you allowed to be alone with your baby sister for brief moments?"

"Yes."

"So, does it make sense your mother would leave you alone with your sister if you continually punched her?"

Akira wrings her hands. "I don't know. But Annie throws that memory in my face all the time."

No wonder Akira allows her sister to mistreat her. "What does your dad remember about that stage in your life?"

"He was working all the time. He didn't know what was going on at home."

"I'm ninety-nine percent sure your mom would have told him when he came home from work. You should ask him."

"He's not going to know," she says in a forlorn voice.

"This is a core memory for you. It would be helpful for you to use your own money to see a counselor who specializes in these kinds of issues. You're twenty-seven years old. You don't need your dad's approval."

Akira pooh-poohs the idea. "I saw a counselor a few times, and our whole family did a couple of family counseling sessions. Annie acted so bad that the counselor refused to see her again."

"That was only one counselor."

"We also saw a psychologist. Same thing happened."

I'm feeling frustrated, but I know God will provide me with the proper tools to secure a positive outcome. "You need to talk to your dad and gain clarity. Do you want me to be with you or can you do this yourself?"

"I'm scared."

"What do you think will happen?"

"Dad will get mad at me."

"For asking a question?"

"He's not going to know the answer."

Why is she so insistent of his ignorance? "There's only one way to find out."

As if on cue, my doorbell rings.

Akira's dad stands on the front stoop. Akira's car is in the repair shop, and he's swung by my house to pick her up.

I usher Mark into the house. "Glass of water?"

He nods. As I start toward the kitchen, I give Akira a meaningful glance.

"Uh, Dad? I have a question."

I place the glass of water on the card table and take a seat. Mark looks at Akira expectantly as he joins us at the table. "What's up?"

Akira breathes in deeply. "Do you remember how I used to punch Annie when she was a baby? You and Mom were scared I would really hurt her?"

Mark sips the water. "You never punched Annie, Akira," he says calmly, "but your sister was pretty violent as a toddler. She'd knock over her little table and chair."

"But Mom had to lock Annie's bedroom door so I couldn't get in."

"Mom locked Annie's door so she couldn't hurt you," says Mark.

He excuses himself to use the bathroom.

I grin. "How do you feel now?"

"Shocked. I've been living a lie all these years."

"You realize Annie was a toddler, not a baby, at that time?"

Akira nods. "I would have been four years old, though still in diapers."

Don't step into that minefield, I tell myself. "If this memory about Annie is false, just consider how many more memories might be based on lies?"

"I let Annie bully me all these years because I thought I deserved to be punished for hurting her," Akira laments.

"Better you found out late than never, right?"

"I guess," she says.

"We all breathe in the truths our parents and siblings tell us. Those truths influence our self-esteem."

Akira still appears dazed. It will take a while for her to come to terms with the fact that she is deserving of love and positive attention.

New Beginnings

WHEN AKIRA WALKS INTO my home office, I can tell she's feeling out of sorts. Her hair is greasy, her acne is acting up, and she's hunched over. I ask if she wants to skip the talking and focus on her writing today, but she shakes her head. I ask if she's started to see the flexible-fee counselor I found for her. She shakes her head again.

"What you need is to make some friends," I tell her.

"I have lots of friends," she protests.

"I'm not talking about your anime online gaming friends. I'm talking about real live friends you can hang out with."

"I am pretty lonely," she concedes.

"How about your autism support group?"

"I get sick every time we get together. I felt anxious, even with the Xanax."

"You don't have to confine yourself to an autism group. Let's see if we can find you a twenty-something Meetup group."

Akira picks at her face. "I don't know if I'm ready."

"When Rocky and I first moved to North Carolina, we joined a Meetup group that introduced us to new people and new activities. It really took away that lonely feeling, especially at holiday time."

Akira looks pensive.

"Humor me."

"Fine."

We hop online and find a twenty-something Meetup group; their Halloween pumpkin-carving event pops on the screen. "How about this?" I ask.

"Sounds interesting," Akira says.

"So let's get you registered."

"Um, I have to check my schedule."

"Do you have anything else going on Saturday nights?" I tease.

"I watch cartoons on TV from twelve a.m. to three a.m."

"There's twenty-one hours before that."

"The truth is, I'm scared," Akira blurts.

"Scared of what?"

"Scared they won't like me. Scared I'll go and nobody will talk to me. Scared I'll have an anxiety attack and humiliate myself."

I breathe in deeply.

"I have to run it by Dad."

"Your dad will be happy to see you go out and enjoy yourself."

"I'm more comfortable with people who have interests the same as me."

"That's why we're focusing on your age group."

"But I don't have the same interests other twenty-seven-year-olds have. They're into drinking, dancing, and partying. I'm into gaming, anime, and animals. I don't drink. I bowl gutters. I'm not good at volleyball."

"They probably have lots of other activities you'll enjoy."

"I can't do it," she protests again.

"Are you sure?" I ask. "Because the Akira I know volunteers in the community, attends Toastmasters, goes to Temple, and enjoys writing."

"Those things don't count because you do those activities with me."

Now was the moment for some tough love. "Do you want to feel this isolated for the rest of your life?"

"No," she mumbles.

"Then you need to make a couple of real live friends you can hang out with."

I pick up the phone. "Let's call your dad and ask him what he thinks."

Mark's voice rings through the loudspeaker. "I think this group could benefit Akira, as long as she takes her Xanax first. She and I will discuss it."

I glance at Akira. "Discuss it tonight?" I mouth.

Akira shakes her head. "I don't know when."

I click off with Mark and turn to Akira. "Look, I'd go with you, but it would look pretty weird having a life coach old enough to be your mother accompanying you to a twenty-something event. You just need to find one person you like in this group. Then you'll have someone to go with you the next time."

"I'll think about it," she says.

"At least sign up for the pumpkin carving party. If you do decide to go, you'll be all set."

Akira shrugs, but she completes the online RSVP.

"If you'd like, I can contact the Meetup organizer and ask her to meet you at the door when you arrive," I suggest. "Better yet, you can do that online yourself."

"We'll see."

"That's fine," I concede. I'm being pushy, but no family member is making an effort to propel this young woman forward. The next step is hers to make.

That night I receive a call from Akira. "What's up?"

Akira's voice is teary. "While Dad, Annie, her boyfriend, and I were at dinner, I mentioned that I had signed up for the event. Annie wasn't too keen on me going."

"What did she say?"

"'The invite said bring a drink. You know they're going to try to get you to drink, right?'

"I knew that the BYO didn't mean sodas, but I was certain that since we would be carving pumpkins they wouldn't get hammered. Beer and sharp cutlery don't make for a good event.

"Annie proceeds to tell me that she had done research on this Meetup group and thought I wouldn't fit in. 'You're just setting yourself up to have a horrible time, and you're going to come home crying.'"

Yet another one of her sister's attempts to shrink Akira down to size. "How did you respond?"

"I just told her I was going. If they were drinking, this would be the only event of theirs I would attend."

Joy surges through my veins at the news. "You really are

beginning to stand up for yourself. How do you feel about how you handled that interaction?"

"It makes me feel a little bit hopeful that I can stand up to my sister again."

Akira's voice now sounds more self-assured.

One more small step forward.

Carving Pumpkins

AKIRA ASSUMES I MUST confidently walk into my own *Moments of Truth* events, as I have encouraged her to do via the Meetup group. Sounds like a reasonable assumption since I've delivered a vast number of speeches at teachers' conferences, writers' conferences, and Toastmasters International contests. But we all know what the first three letters of *assume* spells. In new social situations, as well as presentations, I do experience the jitters.

As a former freelance journalist, I find one-on-one conversations easiest. When I focus on what makes another person tick, as well as what interests we both share, I feel curious, not scared. This is the concept I attempt to impart to Akira. Listening, however, is only half the pie. The other half is sharing similar personal experiences.

My own Achilles heel is that I can't do trivial chit-chat. If I land in one of those situations, I quickly excuse myself after two or three verbal exchanges. Fortunately, most people I encounter quickly get down and dirty in our conversations, and I'm not talking about sex.

I suspect it's because people are flattered when others show a real interest in them. In our daily lives, we ask someone "How are you?" as a mere formality. Usually, we don't hang around long enough to hear the answer *behind* the answer. So when somebody actually focuses on us, we feel special.

At today's session, Akira proudly tells me she attended the

Halloween pumpkin carving Meetup event.

"Tell me everything," I say. "First, how did your emotions in the days leading up to the event mesh with how you felt once you arrived?"

"I was anxious about how I'd get there, since I don't like to drive at night, and I worried about running out of time to buy a pumpkin. I was concerned about how people would react to me—if they'd be rude like Annie. The night of the party came and I was even more nervous than before, but I went anyway."

"Great. You broke through your fear." Akira now understands most clichés.

Akira grins. "I got a nice sized pumpkin at Harris Teeter and had it sitting in my lap as Dad drove me to the party. Since it was thirty minutes away and at night, I decided it would be best for him to give me a lift.

"They didn't really need to know that I was driven by my dad. He and I came up with a reason for me to use: I was going to tell them my car was in the shop and I had gotten a lift from my friend."

"A solid plan," I say.

"We arrived at the address I had been texted. The hostess didn't want random people showing up unannounced at her house so she had asked us to text her if we were attending.

"It was a two story, old colonial-looking building with a fenced-in yard. I thought it was a nice house.

"Walking up to the front door I saw a sign saying to go to the back door. I walked over to the gate and waved goodbye to Dad. I had difficulty getting the gate open. I had to reposition the pumpkin like a football until I could pull the gate open enough for me to squeeze through."

"How did it go once you arrived?"

"I was greeted by a young woman who was checking her phone. There were two tables and a boom box near her. Both tables had a bowl on them and were littered with pumpkin carving supplies.

"'Hey, I'm Gale, and you are?'"

"I signed up on Meetup as Ali, but you can call me Akira. Honestly, either name is fine."

"'Right. You're the new member. This your first time coming to one of these?'"

"I nodded as I placed my pumpkin on the table.

"Gale didn't mind I was early, and the two of us opened the kits for the pumpkins. I borrowed an orange permanent marker and drew a howling wolf on my pumpkin.

"We chatted a bit as more people arrived. I introduced myself a few times as I worked on carving a lid on my pumpkin. Counting Gale's boyfriend, there were ten of us. Everyone was really nice.

"One person, an Egyptian who was here on an internship, had never carved a pumpkin before. I expected the group to be rude and laugh, but instead they all walked him through how to gut and clean it."

"Awesome," I say. "What about the drinking situation?"

"My sister warned me that everybody would be trying to get me drunk, but she was wrong. People were drinking sweet tea and lemonade.

"Gale had cupcakes, cookies, two pizzas, and a plastic pumpkin which she filled with assorted candy as snacks."

"Who else did you chat with at the party?"

"This guy named Alex. We talked about our pets, previous Halloween events, and our pumpkins. I'm not sure how but somehow my carving ended up a cross between the howling wolf I had drawn and the Thunder Cats symbol from the old cartoon. Alex and everyone else were impressed with my artistic talent. Then again, one guy carved a perfect Bronco's symbol into his.

"Toward the end of the party, I moved over to the bonfire pit. It was cold out, and a few people were over there chatting. I ended up with a face full of smoke, which fogged up my glasses and made me cough. We all had a good laugh about that and moved our chairs out of the wind stream so that we didn't get it in our faces.

"At one point, I went into the house because I was getting overstimulated. I sat in the sunroom and talked with the hostess's boyfriend for a while. I told him I was autistic. He said, 'That's cool.'"

"How did his reaction make you feel?"

"Like I really fit in. I signed up for another event next month."

"How long did the party last?" I ask.

"The party went on for three hours, and by nine-thirty, I was starting to grow tired. I phoned Dad and asked if he could come get me. He said he'd be on his way and that it would take about an hour and forty-five minutes. I agreed and sat by the fire chatting about different things with the people there."

"Bravo. You conquered your fears—once again!"

Akira laughs. "It was a fun party, and I talked Dad's ear off with stories on the way home. I can easily see myself going to another event of theirs."

Success.

Talking to Her Younger Self

AKIRA AND I SIT cross-legged on my living room carpet. It's one of those frigid, rainy days when all you want to do is cuddle up with the dogs and drink hot chocolate, both of which we're doing. Today's coaching menu also features one of my famous cement-blasting sessions; at this point in my professional relationship with Akira, I will know when to ease up.

My initial question is innocuous. "Who had your back growing up?"

Akira pauses to reflect. "I only remember times when they didn't have my back, like when I'd tell my parents I was running away to be alone, and they never came after me."

Hm. Not innocuous, after all.

I look at her quizzically.

"When I was ten years old, I thought about ending my life," she confesses. "In my mind, I felt I wasn't worth being around. I felt useless, worthless, and overall someone who would be better off dead. I've never been fond of admitting that I attempted to end it all."

"What made you feel like ending your life?"

"I got into an argument with my mom over how she wasn't sticking up for me against my sister's verbal abuse. I told Mom I doubted she and Annie would miss me if I was dead.

"Then I ran into the kitchen, took a large steak knife from the kitchen, and barricaded myself in my room with it. The worst part was that I actually nicked myself before dropping the knife. I bawled my eyes out for several hours with no sign of Mom, Dad, or my sister coming to comfort me."

My eyes widen.

"You're surprised because I seem like such a happy, upbeat person, right?" she asks.

I smile wanly. The adjectives Akira chooses to describe herself would *never* have crossed my mind. "I'm honored that you're divulging this darkness in your past with me."

Akira nods.

I guide her through some deep breathing exercises. "Now close your eyes and tell me what you remember about ten-year-old Akira."

"My sister and the kids at school called me retard, stupid, dumb. I felt a knot in my chest with each word. Each word still stings when I say it."

Now I'm concerned. "Is your chest or arm hurting?"

Eyes still closed, she shakes her head. "It isn't the kind of knot you get when you're nervous. It's more like a dull pain where you don't know what to do and feel like crap. I honestly can say I felt unprotected and unwanted."

"When you ran away, did your parents come looking for you?"

"The farthest I got away from the house was a third of a mile down the street to a friend's house. Otherwise I ran into the parking lot of the college near my house.

"I would usually be gone half an hour or more, crying my eyes out with no one there to comfort me. I do remember one time a campus police officer pulled up and asked 'Are you lost?' A ten-year-old girl does not look like she belongs on a college campus at night.

"I told him I wasn't lost and then pointed in the direction I had come from, telling him my house was a short five-minute trek from there and I could get home fine."

"How did your parents react when you returned home?"

"They didn't hug or comfort me. They hadn't even called the cops thinking I may have been kidnapped. All I got was a simple 'Where were you?'"

"Did your family ever sit you down with you to discuss why you were so angry and sad?"

"Nothing."

"How did their non-reaction make you feel?"

"Like my thoughts and feelings meant nothing. My parents didn't even think to follow me and that pissed me off. What kind of parent does that? Usually when I ran away to the campus, students were going to their cars, drinking, smoking, or starting fights."

"Did your parents send you to a therapist or do family counseling?"

Akira shakes her head. "Not until I was in my late teens. I always wondered why not. If my daughter or son tried to commit suicide or run away, I would send them to a therapist or a psychiatrist as soon as possible. Suicide attempts and running away are pleas for help."

This conversation has derailed into something I'm not equipped to handle. "Have you discussed this stuff with your new social worker?"

Akira shakes her head. "The couple of times I've seen her, it's never come up."

"These are issues you really need to explore with her."

"I'm not sure I can talk about it with anybody—except you."

Multiple times, I have asked Akira to resume seeing her social worker through the Jewish Federation. She promises to do so, but the following week, she's always got an excuse for not going.

Maybe I can delve just a wee bit deeper. "Who did you turn to for help?"

"I had no friends to speak of, no adult to turn to, not even religious school teachers. My former rabbi wasn't the warm, hugging kind of guy that the two rabbis here are. He was more the kind to say 'thank you for coming to services' and leave it at that."

"How about your Aunt Marley?"

"During the time I was feeling miserable, Aunt Marley lived in another state, so she couldn't physically comfort me. I don't know why I didn't try to call her about any of this. Maybe I was afraid of how she'd view me."

"View you?"

"Like I caused all this pain for my family."

I am stunned. "You thought you were to blame?"

Akira nods.

"Let's try something different. Close your eyes, breathe in, breathe out."

Akira does as I instruct.

"See the younger you. What is she doing? How is she dressed? Greet her and tell her you're sorry you couldn't rescue her but you didn't have the strength back then to protect her. Tell her now that you are grown up, you will be her knight in shining armor."

Then Akira speaks. "She says that's all bullshit."

"Explain to your younger self that you value her. Tell her about all you've accomplished as an adult, that her life doesn't end there. This is what she has to look forward to."

Akira once again closes her eyes and is silent. Then she replies. "I told her we were not useless, not worthless. Certainly not someone who should end it all. We deserved to live."

"Does she believe you?"

Akira shakes her head. "She's skeptical that our life really changed."

"At least you told her, and she heard it."

Akira sweeps her hair away from her face. "I guess."

"Who has your back now that you're an adult?"

Akira ticks off names on one hand. "My online gaming friends. All of them are awesome and we get along like a big family. Then there's Damon and Aunt Marley."

I stifle a groan. Damon lives five thousand miles away; her aunt is five states away.

"Besides being my life coach, you're one of my best friends. I feel like I can vent my ball of rage at you without being judged. And your husband thinks of me as an honorary daughter, which is very sweet. He even offered me one of his canes when my legs got shaky during Yom Kippur services.

"If I'd had that kind of support group when I was young, my self-esteem might be higher today. I wouldn't have run away from home for attention or thought I was a worthless human being."

"How do your online gaming friends make you feel they've got your back?" I ask.

Akira smiles for the first time this session. "I'm in an online guild, which is a group of five or more members. We go on World of Warcraft missions to retrieve dangerous objects and put them away for safekeeping. Currently, we're hunting for a book that could prove extremely valuable to our cause.

"In my first roleplay event with them, I failed an escape roll not once but three times. You have to roll a ten or over to succeed in the action. My first roll was to get across a waterway. Another guild member and I both failed that roll and got stuck in the muddy water.

"We rolled again to try and free ourselves. She succeeded in getting free while my character, a troll druid, failed and unfortunately managed to alert a sea giant, who oddly enough was blind to the fact that we were here. The giant started coming my way, hearing me splash around trying to free my feet.

"At this point, everyone began to freak out. They knew if the sea giant found me, I was toast. I attempted a third roll and yet again failed. This resulted in me being picked up by the sea giant and dropped into a fiery dragon pit. My team had the choice of going off to fight or rescue my character from a fiery dragon pit.

"As I was being carried away by the sea giant, I yelled out to the guild, 'Find the book. It's worth more than my life.'

"A member who plays my character's brother went ballistic at the thought of losing me, despite my urging the guild to focus on the mission and forget about me. He began to cuss out the sea giant, calling it an overgrown sushi roll.

"In a 180-degree turn, the whole guild went to emergency rescue mission. I couldn't believe they would suddenly drop the mission for a valued item just to save me, a newbie. A mock battle ensued, and after several turns, they successfully saved my butt. I was amazed they had gone to the trouble to rescue me."

"Why were you so surprised?" I ask.

"They had a choice of rescuing one character or going to war to save a large number. In previous guilds, they wouldn't think twice about leaving a fallen comrade behind. I'm actually happy to know that this guild has a 'leave no member behind' kind of mentality. Being treated like a valued member really makes someone with low self-esteem feel like they belong."

"Do you feel you're not worth saving in real life, too?" I ask gently.

Akira considers this question. Then she nods.

"In Judaism, if you save one life, it's as if you've saved the world," I remind her.

"But it's not like I'm a doctor or a scientist who can help humanity," she says.

"Each person's life is equally as precious as the other. Money, power, education, none of that matters. God made each of us with the spark of the Divine within."

"I guess," she says doubtfully.

"So what happened once you were saved?" I ask.

"At the end of the event, my character got down on her knees in the wet sand and repeatedly apologized to the guild leader for them having to change course.

"The leader responded with something that brought tears to my eyes. 'As long as you're safe and no one died, that's all that matters.'

"Now I know my online friends have my back and would jump at the chance to punch out my enemies' lights."

"You know, there are a lot of people who care about you

besides those you mentioned." I begin to enumerate. "The folks at the Jewish Federation and the Temple. Your boss at PetSmart, who gave you six weeks of unpaid medical leave after your surgery, even though she wasn't required to do so. What about when Toastmasters gave you that fruit lollipops basket after you got out of the hospital? All these people can't be wrong."

"I don't want to talk about this stuff anymore today."

I nod. She must be emotionally exhausted. "Our time for today is up, anyway."

I walk Akira out to her car. "Know what's cool?"

She turns to face me. "What?"

"You were able to assert yourself with me just now, when you felt you'd reached your limit."

Akira grins as she slips behind the wheel. "You're not just my life coach, you're like family."

My grin is as wide as hers as I walk back up my driveway.

For Love of a Dog

Akira flips open her newest journal entry. She is obsessed about finding the key to unlock her sister's soul. "If only I knew the right thing to say to Annie or the right gift to give her so she'd know I love her and stop treating me so mean."

She begins to read aloud to me from For Love of a Dog: Soothing My Sister's Soul:

> *Sunday rolled around and I asked Dad if he wanted to go to the adoption fair called Bark and Wine. Annie has been looking for a dog for a while. I thought after my last failed attempt involving the animal shelter, I might have better luck there.*
>
> *"I want to go. Maybe we can help Annie find her perfect pup," I told him.*
>
> *Dad agreed and we got in the car. When we arrived at the fair, the two of us got wristbands and proceeded to walk around.*
>
> *There were booths ranging from vendors, to food, to adoption agencies. Dad got a mango slushie while I got a blue raspberry one. I love blue raspberry but getting slushies was not why we were here.*
>
> *I managed to find Annie and her boyfriend by one of the wine booths and asked what she was*

looking for in a dog so I would have better luck finding one for her.

"Male, maximum of a year old, no bully breeds, medium size, a golden or poodle mix."

I knew Annie was dead set on a goldendoodle or labradoodle puppy. Hopefully I could find one that fit the bill.

After walking around for a good hour in the blistering heat, my eyes landed on what looked like a golden retriever mix. Lucky me! The dog was wearing the bandana that said Adopt Me on it.

"Wow, I think I just found my sister's perfect dog. Can you tell me about her?"

"She's a foster we've had for a week. Her owner had to go to the hospital and is now unable to care for her. She's a golden retriever, cocker spaniel mix. She's about a year old. Very lovable, energetic, and a bit shy around new dogs."

I broke into a huge grin. According to what the foster mom said about Lucy, which was the dog's name, she fit all but one of Annie's requirements. I quickly introduced myself and mentioned my sister was looking for a dog. I also mentioned about our own dog Misty and explained a bit about her.

The woman gave me a card and I thanked her for letting me see Lucy. I rushed over and told Annie. She was impressed that the dog was from a shelter she knew about called Red Dog Farm.

The two of us went to track down Lucy so my sister could see her. We found them near the Red Dog Farm booth.

One look into Lucy's eyes and Annie was smitten.

"Did I do a good job?"

"Are you kidding? She's absolutely perfect, Akira. Way to go."

Annie gave me a high five and a big grin of happiness. I had found her perfect dog and felt like I was on top of the world.

"Hey, you gave me a list of what you were looking for. That helped a ton."

"Awesome job, Akira. I'm glad you found her."

She quickly filled out an adoption application with the assistance of the volunteers. It turned out Lucy had one other potential adopter. From what we were told by the foster mom, the person had said they were going to call about Lucy.

The four of us went home shortly after, since the heat was getting too much for us.

Tuesday night rolled around, and I got a text from Annie saying that they had a doggy meeting Friday between Lucy and Misty. They had gotten through the most stressful part in our minds.

Misty has a few health problems so we were worried that might throw a wrench in the adoption. It didn't, and I began getting pictures and videos from Annie that the foster mom had taken.

I can't believe that a dog adoption would be the key to getting Annie to treat me with respect. It's been almost a full week, and she's been asking my advice about toys and food for Lucy. She usually shoots down any comments or suggestions I offer. This is a complete one-hundred-eighty from how she usually acts toward me. I'm starting to wonder if alien pooches have abducted my sister.

I did a little research to see what they might

look for that would cause Annie not to get Lucy. It was mostly aggressive behavior between the dogs.

Both Lucy and Misty get shy around new dogs, but Dad assured the both of us that Misty and Lucy would do fine at their meeting. I sure hope he's right.

This dog is absolutely perfect for Annie and Alfie so I really hope the meeting Friday goes well.

"So you think you finally can participate in a safe relationship with Annie?" I ask.

"She's being a lot nicer to me now," says Akira. "I'm using my PetSmart discount to buy her dog food and a harness, too."

Although I have my doubts about her sister's motives, it's a respite Akira well deserves. "I'm so glad. Let's just hope this feeling of good will continues."

Continuing with Toastmasters

AKIRA CONTINUES TO ATTEND Toastmasters with me on a weekly basis. She still clutches the podium upon rising to speak, and her voice is still way too quiet; however, she has willingly assumed a variety of leadership roles toward her Competent Leader Certificate. These roles include toastmaster, timer, grammarian, word master, and filler-words counter. The important thing is she's beginning to feel accepted and not judged for being autistic. Everyone in the club is very encouraging to her.

To date, Akira has given five out of a possible ten speeches, each five to seven minutes in duration. She's also chaired the Christmas party and won best speaker three times. Two of those times, she bested two area contest winners, one of them being me. That was a shocker for both of us! Next, she hopes to win the humorous speech contest at the club and area levels.

Given all Akira's accomplishments, I am disappointed when she refuses to attend our Toastmasters Spring Conference at a hotel ten minutes from her house.

"I'm still getting used to driving on the expressway," she hedges.

"It's not on a highway," I say stubbornly. "It's on a main road."

"I don't know anybody there. I'll have an anxiety attack and embarrass myself."

"All you have to do is listen to people give five-minute speeches and applaud, and I'm going to be one of the contestants!"

"Yeah—but what if I make a fool of myself?"

"I'm presenting a humorous speech about me, a homeowner/realtor, showing my own house while my three dogs yap away and I fall into a puddle of dog pee. You're worried about making a fool of yourself? Whatever. You don't have to come if you don't want to."

"I do want to go . . . I'm just scared. I feel bad not going because it would be a good networking situation to help me improve my speeches more, but I think I'll take a raincheck on this one."

"Fine," I say.

After we click off our phones, I recall an old saying: "You can't want it more than your client." I need to allow Akira to mature at her own pace, not mine.

Chastened, I phone her back. "I'm proud of you for standing up to me, an authority figure. You've made leaps and bounds since we first met. You'll know when you're ready to move forward."

It is the day before the Toastmaster's division contest, to be held thirty minutes away. Once again, I phone and invite Akira to attend with me.

"It's a bit early in the morning for me," she hedges. "I sleep late on Saturdays."

"No excuses!" I remind her.

"I'll try to make it to see you compete."

I reply as if she'd never said that horrible word *try* and instead said *will*. "Great. Drive over to my house at 8:00 a.m. We'll take two cars, in case you feel the need to leave early."

"Okay," she grunts. Obviously not a happy camper.

Lots of road construction next morning, but we finally make it to the church hosting the event. The parking lot is packed. Akira texts me, worried about parking in the tiny spaces. "Hopefully I can squeeze my tiny Camry into a spot with minimal adjustments," she says. This is the third time I've noticed Akira's skewed perception of size. Her car is a four-door, mid-sized vehicle.

I emerge from my car and use arm gestures to guide her into an adjacent space. After Akira parks, we make our way into the church and follow the signs to the auditorium. Today's contestants sit in the front row and everyone else sits behind them. I slip into a seat next to a middle-aged man who looks like a nice person. Corey, the president in our Toastmaster's group, sits behind me. At least there is one person I know.

The speakers draw lots and the contest began. My dog-sitting speech causes Akira to laugh so hard, she's crying. She's dog sat for me before, so she knows my pooches can be "hyper balls of fluff," as she refers to them.

While the judges are evaluating our speeches, we contestants are allowed time to chat with the audience. I'm pleased to note that Akira is complimenting a few of the speakers.

Unfortunately, I do not place in this contest because I "performed" my speech rather than spoke it. Afterwards, Akira offers an interesting insight. "The fact you stuck dirty socks in the freezer next to the popsicles to hide them last minute made my stomach churn. I understand finding an emergency hiding place as well as the next guy, but hiding them in the freezer and then offering the potential buyer popsicles probably wasn't the smartest idea."

I burst out laughing. "The popsicles and muddy socks incident never actually happened."

"Oh!"

Still with the literal thinking.

Later, she says she asked a couple of speakers about their opinions on entering one of her own speeches in a future contest. "I think a speech about things that can happen to a PetSmart associate would be amusing. They thought it was clever how I described going on a rescue mission for a hamster, and two people asking for baby bottles and formula for newborn squirrels. Maybe I'll enter the next contest and pray to the PetSmart gods!"

"That will be great," I say.

Although I didn't place in the division contest, I am thrilled Akira came out of her shell long enough to socialize. What an accomplishment!

Social Security

Akira plops down in a card table chair across from mine. "We won!" she says. "My social security advocate said that ninety-nine percent of cases don't find out the verdict until months later, but my judge said, 'I think you'll be happy with my verdict.'"

After three years of roadblocks, Akira just found out she will receive social security. While the majority of Americans only receive SSI after they turn sixty-five, there are certain chronic mental or physical health conditions which enable a younger person to receive these benefits.

According to Akira's legal advocate, a person who is diagnosed with autism before age twenty-two and has written proof of that diagnosis is allowed to apply for SSI. Akira pulls her journal from her purse. "I actually wrote a new entry. Want to hear it?"

"Of course," I say.

> *It was Friday morning and Dad, who was going to be a witness in my case, got up early. The case was to be held at nine forty-five a.m. Connie, my social security advocate, told us to get there an hour early. Sometimes the courthouse runs late with cases.*
>
> *Dad and I got in the car and drove to the location. I was shaking and unsure of what would be asked of me. I hadn't been told a huge amount*

of what to expect. Dad thought we'd be fine. We then agreed that if he was to testify, I would leave the room so he could vent without stressing me out. I knew Dad had a ton of stuff he kept hidden from me.

We arrived on time and walked through the security checkpoint. The alarm went off—on my pants, no less—like it did when I had jury duty. I will never understand how a tiny piece of metal is enough to set off the alarm. Dad luckily did not set the alarm off.

The two of us took the elevator to the third floor and met up with Connie to go to the conference room. I was given a briefing before walking in about what the layout would look like. There was a long wooden table in the room with microphones at three spots. At one end was myself and at the other end was the judge's booth. Connie sat to my left and the court reporter was on my right. Dad sat by the wall behind Connie.

I was asked my name, age, who I lived with, and current job. It was pretty much a repeat of the jury interview I had prior. Nothing too major. However, I was asked to speak louder so the microphone could pick up my voice.

The judge then asked me a few more questions about autism and why I believed I was deserving of SSI.

"Specifically?" I asked.

"How does autism affect your social interactions? What do you do when you're not working at PetSmart? Why do you think you should get SSI?"

Akira continues to read from her entry:

I used the skills I learned in Toastmasters and treated it like a round of table topics. It made things easier for me and I was certain I had answered the questions to the best of my abilities.

"That is all I need. Case closed."

"Wait? Don't you need my dad to testify?"

"I have what I need. I believe you will appreciate my verdict."

Connie, Dad, and I looked at each other a moment. The judge didn't need to hear my dad vent? This was unexpected.

The three of us got up and left the room to reconvene by the elevator. I was starting to shake a bit. It wasn't an anxiety attack, though. More an adrenaline rush from giving my all to winning our case.

"Akira, congratulations," Connie told me.

I looked confused so she proceeded to explain that we had won the case and that she would keep us informed as the rest of the case rolled out. We all left with grins on our faces.

Inwardly, I was doing autistic flappy arms and dancing around like a dog wearing booties; outwardly, I was smiling and calm. After four years, we reached the finish line.

"Why did it take so long for you to be approved for SSI benefits?" I ask.

"I didn't have a car. They didn't know my mom had passed away. They needed my pay stubs to prove I was working under twenty-eight hours per week and have less than two thousand dollars in my bank account."

Akira says it will take seven months to a year to start receiving funds. I am so happy for her.

Computer Upgrade

After completing our goals for today's session, Akira mentions she needs to upgrade her computer to one that "won't fry an egg on the keyboard after half an hour of gaming."

One of the innate characteristics of life coaching I value is the freedom to spread our wings at the whim of the wind. Still, that whim needs to be voiced by the client, not by me. "Would you prefer another cooking lesson or checking out a new gaming computer?" I ask.

Akira takes a moment to consider my question. "My current laptop has reached its final days. It runs even the simplest applications real slow. On top of that, it has begun to overheat when I play a simple game like Minecraft. It's time I get an upgraded gaming computer."

Yes! I enjoy getting out of the office!

We choose Best Buy as our destination. As we zip off in my car, I ask why a special computer is needed to play games.

"A gamer's computer needs to be a well-oiled *vehicle* that can run just about anything without being restricted," says Akira. "Keeping a car for ten plus years is fine because they are built to last for 300,000 miles, but game graphics become obsolete on a monthly basis. These days, my laptop runs more like a tricycle with three flat tires than a V8 Chevy SS in a NASCAR race. This makes gaming very difficult because my graphics card can't render textures and movement fast enough."

Okay, then.

Finding the computer/electronics section is easy. There's a glowing blue sign on the wall reading *Windows*, along with the symbol for the console. I notice an off-brand for cheap and point to the touch screen laptop. "How about this one?"

Akira pales and rapidly shakes her head. "Damon had that brand and it broke several times within a year. It got to the point it was in the shop more than it was on his desk. Too many issues with the hardware, if you ask me."

Next, a couple of Alienware and Acer computers on the other table. "How about these?" I ask.

"I used Alienware when I was in college. As much as I'd love an Alienware, check out the price tag. I have a somewhat limited budget. Also, I don't need a computer with all the bells and whistles."

I beckon a computer associate to help Akira find a computer to meet her gaming specs. Akira has already disappeared down the laptop aisle and is engrossed in reading various specs. The associate mentions gaming computers range from $599 to $2,000. The three of us stand before a fifteen-inch monitor flanked by a glowing red keyboard. I love red. "Get this one," I urge.

"As long as it can run World of Warcraft without overheating I'm set," Akira says.

The customer sales associate produces the specs: 16 gigabytes, 15-inch monitor, two designated graphic cards, for a grand total of $1,190.

I presume this purchase to be a slam-dunk when Akira throws a curve ball. "I need to run it by my dad first."

"Best Buy is running a promo," I tell her. "You don't need to pay for this computer in one lump sum. You can pay it off monthly with zero percent interest for twelve months."

"Based on what your down-payment is, your monthly fee may be as low as $67," says the associate.

"That's actually not bad considering I only make about $400 a month before taxes," says Akira.

I encourage Akira to sign up right there and then, but she isn't quite ready to get a new computer just yet. "I have to figure out what will happen with my old laptop before I invest in a new computer. I'm also worried how Dad would react to me spending a thousand dollars on a new computer when, in his mind, my current one still works."

"Your dad's not paying for this computer, you are," I say. "You need to make your own decisions."

"I guess breaking out from under Dad's thumb still hasn't set in completely. But this is a big step for me, a decision I can't take lightly."

Akira is thinking about doing a trade-in, so we speak to the geek squad. Sure enough, they tell her she can do so if the old computer is in good condition. They advise her to check the HP website to make sure.

"How do you want to proceed?" I ask her.

"I am going to sleep on it and wait to see if there are any cheaper options for a new laptop. There are still too many unknown variables I have to get squared away."

As I drop Akira off at her house, I commend her on how effectively she dealt with the computer sales associate, the geek squad associate, and me. "In each instance, you voiced your needs and opinions and refused to act until you examined all your options.

You're beginning to trust your gut, rather than going along with authority figures, even when that authority figure is me."

Akira gives me a half smile. "This is exhausting."

I grin. "Life's lessons always are."

A couple of days after our shopping adventure, Akira phones to tell me her dad showed her a Lenovo gaming computer online that exceeds her expectations. "This was after he told me it was an absurd waste of money to buy a new computer because I lacked the funds. His premise was laughable because I have more than enough money in my bank account to pay upfront for the computer."

"Tell me everything," I say.

"Actually, I wrote a journal entry. Want to hear it?"

Akira now writes journal entries without my prodding. Another milestone met. "Sure!" I say.

> *"Walking in the door, I found my dad sitting on the couch with our dog Misty. He was on his work laptop checking emails and replying to messages from coworkers.*
>
> *"What did you and Jennie do today?" Dad asked.*
>
> *"We went to Best Buy to look at laptops."*
>
> *"Akira, you don't have the money to drop on a new computer," he said.*
>
> *"Dad, I make my own money and they have a monthly plan based on how much you put down."*
>
> *"You still don't make enough to buy a computer. You didn't get one, did you?"*
>
> *I felt like my heart had been torn in half. Here*

I was telling my dad what we had done, and he goes and gets upset with me. I thought he would have been happy I was taking the initiative to get a better system instead of relying on him.

"No, I chose to wait because I wasn't sure what to do with the one I have now."

"Bring it downstairs and we'll run a diagnostic on it."

Fifteen minutes, four diagnostic tests, and two arguments later, Dad finally agreed that my computer should not be running this slowly. He looked annoyed about the entire ordeal. He even went so far as to say he needed to put a parental lock on my computer so I couldn't download unknown programs without his knowledge.

Those programs were given to me by Damon, who uses them on his own computer. One was a junk file remover and the other was a malware remover that caught more viruses than the one the system came with. I knew for a fact that they were valid and worked just fine. The nerve of my dad thinking I would download something I didn't trust.

"Dad, I'm twenty-freaking-eight. I know not to download malicious applications. You asked me what I did with Jennie and I told you. You did not need to snap at me and threaten to put a parental lock on my computer. I'm trying to make independent decisions, but you're putting up a firewall and making it tough for me to do that."

With that said, I stormed up to my room and got on Skype to talk to my friends Luna and Chloe. Both thought my dad was out of line for even suggesting the parental lock. I agreed.

A few days later, my dad surprised me.

He had researched gaming computers. I looked at him in disbelief. One minute he's arguing I don't need a new computer and then he does research on them.

Dad showed me a Lenovo gaming computer's specs on his laptop screen. That was unusual since, in the past when he's gotten me new computers, I had no say in what their specs were. Sure enough, the computer had really good specs. It was miles ahead of what my current laptop and the one we had seen at Best Buy was. I . . . was . . . stunned.

"I picked a 'build your own' and chose some of the higher end add-ons," said Dad. "Does this look like it will cover your gaming needs?"

My jaw dropped in response. Who was this guy and where was my real dad? He had never listened to my arguments in the past.

Showing him how bad my computer had become must have opened his eyes. "Uh, yeah, this looks like a massive upgrade to what I have now."

"Good, grab your debit card and we'll order it."

My card? Wait, I was going to get to pay for this laptop with the money I had in the bank that I previously was told I couldn't use? Dad had to have been abducted by aliens.

I rushed over to my purse, grabbed my wallet, and rushed back. I filled out my information and sent the order in. I made sure to give my work email since it was more professional than my personal email. Within minutes I received an email saying Lenovo had gotten my order and the laptop would be shipped sometime around Chanukah.

A computer that doesn't fry an egg after half an hour? Here I come.

I give Akira a high five. "Way to go! In the end, your dad respected you enough to take your opinion and feelings into consideration."

"I was even more surprised Dad would actually let me pay for a large purchase with my own money," says Akira. "That has never happened before."

"You rock, Akira. You've recognized the more proactive you are in stating your needs with your dad, the better the outcome."

Hair Fiasco

I'VE COACHED AKIRA FOR eighteen months. Only once do I recall her getting a haircut. So when Akira arrives for our weekly coaching session, I surprise her. "How about we get our hair cut today?"

"I really do need to get a good two to three inches whacked off," she says. "I've got split ends and my hair is an overall mess. Plus, the highlights have worn out, and I've got quite a few more silver hairs from dealing with work and Annie."

"Great," I say. "I've got a coupon for Empire beauty school, so let's go there."

Akira stares back at me with that deer-in-the-headlights expression. "Um, I actually have a particular hair stylist I've been going to for the last twelve years."

"It's normal to be anxious if you've never gone to another stylist," I say brightly. "Just look at this as one more new experience. Who knows? You might like the beauty school."

"I don't know."

"Can we at least walk inside and check out what services they provide?"

"Changing routine isn't something many people with autism, Asperger's, or any spectrum disorder enjoy," says Akira. "It causes us huge amounts of unwanted stress and worry. Even the tiniest of changes can throw us straight into an anxiety attack. We become nonverbal or punch, hit, or claw ourselves to try to break free of the anxiety."

"Are you planning to punch, hit, or claw at yourself today?"

Akira's shoulders relax. "No."

Minutes later, we swing open the door leading into the beauty school. Akira is impressed with the bright wooden flooring, warm colors on the walls, and black leather chairs in the lobby. "It honestly looks a lot nicer than where I usually go to get my hair cut."

Unfortunately, the school just finished their afternoon appointments and won't re-open until 5:30 p.m., when the next group of student beauticians arrives. I have another tutoring student at 5:00.

"Maybe we shouldn't have gone out for lunch, then we wouldn't have been late," says Akira. But she sounds relieved.

I consider calling off the whole hair cutting expedition. But when I ask Akira if she wants to give another beauty school a try, she nods. I shove my misgivings aside and drive to the Health and Style Institute.

Akira is the first to spot five feral cats lounging in the forest area that flanks the parking lot. A lazy Susan tray of dry cat food is placed in close proximity to the well-nourished cats. She says spotting animals from a distance comes from working a year at PetSmart and having to be on the lookout for any escapees or human pet parents needing assistance.

She unsuccessfully attempts to entice a beautiful grey and white cat to come hither. "This cat is more interested in hiding in the bushes with some of the others than getting attention from strange, hairless beasts who walk on two feet."

We perform our own meowing rendition; the cats are

unimpressed. We then bid the cats adieu and enter the Institute.

Akira thinks the Institute looks like a storage unit that had been renovated into a beauty parlor. The floor is a large slab of cement and the walls are metal alloy painted in red, silver, and black. "Not the most appealing place to get your hair cut," she says warily, "and this is only the lobby."

By this point, Akira is starting to shake and repeatedly uttering the phrases, "I don't know" and "I'm more used to having Amy cut my hair." She says she's been told, "If your first instinct in a situation is to turn tail and run, do it."

"You can do this, Akira," I say calmly. "Just breathe."

After conversing with the receptionist, we learn the beauty institute has four different student expertise levels, ranging from brand new students to those poised to graduate. We peruse the description booklet, and then request a level three or four to cut our hair. "I'm not about to let someone with no idea what they're doing whack inches off my hair," Akira says.

The receptionist tells us her level three or four students don't come in until 5:30 p.m.

Akira begins to hyperventilate as we debate whether to select a stylist who isn't graduating for six months. The good thing is, haircut prices are less expensive for that group of beauty school students, a fact that impresses me more than Akira.

Then the receptionist offers us three salon and beauty menu items for twenty-five dollars. Bummer. The deal can't be split between two people.

Freaking-out vibes shoot from Akira like porcupine quills. She turns on her heel and makes a beeline for the door, with me following like a baby chick.

Once in the parking lot, she whips out her cell phone from her pocket. "I'm calling Amy."

"How do you know she even still works there?" I ask.

"I don't give a damn if Amy is gone," she says through gritted teeth. "I still trust that place."

"Hi, Amy!" she says into the phone.

"Who is this?"

She puts the phone on loudspeaker. "It's Akira Stone."

"Who again?"

"Ak-ir-a Stone."

"Oh, Akira. How are you? I saw your sister Annie recently and asked her how you were."

Akira raises an eyebrow. "What did Annie say?"

"She said you were good."

"Just good?"

"She didn't say much. So, you need a haircut?"

"Yeah and a wax. It looks like caterpillars growing on my face."

The hair stylist laughs and tells Akira she has an opening for two-thirty on Saturday afternoon.

Akira confirms the appointment and clicks off the phone. "I only trust Amy to cut my hair. I can't wait to see her again."

As we drive home, I say, "I am proud of you for attempting something new. I'm also proud of you for knowing what you can and cannot handle."

Akira gives me a half-smile.

It's been a wacky day, but I am reassured she can be trusted to make sound decisions.

Entrepreneurs!

Although Akira recently celebrated her twenty-eighth birthday, she continues to believe she deserves to be victimized by her sister. As I suspected, Annie had only taken a harassment sabbatical so Akira would give her a PetSmart discount on food and equipment for her new dog.

However, there are signs Akira's self-esteem is beginning to poke its head out of its shell as she connects with her talents and abilities. Thus, I once again nudge my little turtle one tiny claw's step out of her comfort zone.

"Would you be interested in selling your anime drawings at a couple of Temple holiday art fairs?" I ask. Akira has shown a number of congregants her drawings after Shabbat services, and they've appeared interested. The Temple administrator even called them "excellent."

But Akira's got her doubts. "There are lots of artists who are better than me. Besides, not everybody is into Japanese cartoons."

"Are there other arts and crafts you enjoy creating?"

"Not really."

I've found that, even with my very young students, self-actualization and self-esteem are two sides of the same coin. Once these students learn the necessary academic and behavioral skills and see themselves as capable, their self-esteem blossoms. They are then free to actualize their dreams without being bogged down by emotional barriers.

I point to a glittering object on Akira's kitchen counter. "What's this?"

"It's a beaded lizard keychain. The tail is missing because Misty mistook it for a shiny chew toy."

I pick up the slightly chewed object. "Isn't this something elementary school kids make?"

"Well, yes, but even teenagers hook them to their car keys," she says. "I haven't made them in years, but they're still really popular."

"Can you make money selling these things?"

"I've seen pictures on Etsy.com of people displaying their keychains for sale. I just need enough beads to fill an Olympic-sized swimming pool."

I can't recall hearing a person with Asperger's tell a laugh-out-loud joke. "Anything else you know how to make besides lizards?"

At this point, I visualize classy looking beads, i.e. gold and silver.

"My sister has a keychain of a blue clown fish. I could do something like that."

"If you make different objects, you can sell them for different prices," I suggest.

Akira researches and prints seven beaded animal and holiday templates; these include the iconic lizard, a rainbow, penguin, flower chain, another lizard, rainbow, candy corn, dragonfly, and watermelon. "I picked the rainbow because two of my friends are LGBTQ," she says. "I want to do something special to honor them since in college they always stuck up for me when I was being picked on for being Jewish."

The following week, Akira and I scour Michael's Nursery & Crafts and Hobby Lobby to find the appropriate bead colors. The beads reflect the colors of the rainbow—neutrals, glittery shades, and metallic. Akira stares at her options, mentally computing the number of beads per color she needs. The bags range in size from 250 to 500 beads.

"Some of the patterns require over fifty beads in multiple colors, and each bag cost five dollars," she laments.

I show Akira how to compare prices with the number of ounces contained in each bag of beads. My client is like my husband; they choose one store and, once they get there, stick with it, even if it's more expensive. Akira doesn't want to schlep to a different store that has a sale going on, but I urge her to shop and compare—just one more tidbit of consumer education training.

"Afterward, we'll check out Walmart to find the best bang for your buck," I say, patting her on the back.

We continue our exploration. Akira repeatedly reminds me that Perler beads are the wrong kind. "It's like the shiny Perler beads are calling to you to take them home and ignore those other beads, but we need Pony beads," she says.

"What's the difference?" I'm smitten with the glittering colors.

"You run a hot iron over Perler beads to form the pattern. I need the kind you make beaded friendship bracelets with. Perler beads also won't fit on the lanyard."

I finally take the hint and Akira begins pulling bags of different colored Pony beads. Since Akira is doing a rainbow, she grabs red, orange, yellow, blue, green, and purple. To add some extra pop to the rainbows, she adds glittery purple beads. Then she selects black and white beads for the main colors of the penguins. For the lizards, she chooses three bags of neon colored beads in blue, green, and pink.

After extending our search to Walmart to purchase what Akira deems enough beads, we wind up returning to Michael's, where she opens an account in case additional supplies are needed.

By the time we finish shopping, Akira has purchased seven bags totaling four thousand beads and one hundred keychain rings. She already has lanyards at home.

"Your homework is to assemble ten beaded lizards per week," I tell her. "You've got five weeks to produce sixty to seventy keychains to exhibit at the fairs. If you complete ten key chains per week, you won't be overwhelmed at the last minute."

Akira's face drops. "I don't know how many keychains I can finish, because I'm working."

"How many hours are you now working each day?" I ask.

Her eyes turn fiery. "Four hours, three to four times a week!"

I roll my eyes. "That's no excuse. Most people work forty to sixty hours per week!"

"Well, I still have to get home to feed and walk my dog," she persists.

I change the subject. "How much do you plan to charge for each keychain?"

Her voice sinks back to a monotone. "Three dollars."

"It costs fifty dollars to rent vendor space at each fair," I say. "How about charging six dollars per key chain and ten dollars for two keychains?"

"No one is going to spend that much," Akira protests.

"If I'd advertised two houses for the price of one house for sale when I was selling real estate, I would have had a zillion clients! That gimmick always works," I promise.

"I guess I could try," Akira says, dubiously.

"Great. You're demonstrating flexible thinking."

"Annie will say it's a stupid idea."

"It only matters what you think."

Akira manages a half-smile. I give her a reassuring hug.

I've only previewed one of Akira's beaded keychains and have no clue if Akira is capable of producing a marketable product. But I am here to encourage, not squash, her dreams.

I telephone two temples to register us as vendors for their arts & crafts fairs. Akira will sell her beaded keychains while I autograph and sell my mystery novels at the table next to hers.

Later that week, Akira starts working on the keychains. She crafts not ten keychains per week but five keychains per day while sitting on her bedroom floor with the bags scattered around her. As the weeks fly by, Akira produces ten lizards, ten flying bugs, ten watermelons, ten candy corns, ten penguins, and ten rainbows to exhibit at the arts & crafts fairs. Although she hasn't finished in time to sell the keychains at the children's craft fair, Akira is able to exhibit at the Chanukah Extravaganza.

I suggest Akira design a poster to advertise her products, even though she is still hesitant about the two-for-one concept. She names her booth *Firefox's Beaded Treasure*. As a cute idea, she formed the O in the shape of a fox head.

As we enter Temple this frigid December night, Akira is in complaint mode. "My back is sore and my fingers are tingling from making seventy keychains by hand."

Just a testament to my husband's favorite saying: *Life is hard and then you die.* Somehow, I don't think Akira needs to hear that right now.

I pray Akira won't go into panic attack mode in front of the crowd filing into the social hall. Then I remember that several months ago I'd invited Akira to come to Kentucky Derby Day at the Temple. She'd been tentative about attending the event but had gotten more into the spirit of the event as we shopped for her new hat.

The day of the Derby event, a gorgeous young woman walked into the Temple. I initially didn't recognize the face beneath the big floppy hat. Then I realized it was Akira.

She sat down at a table with her dad and did a terrific job conversing with the people next to her. She also seemed just fine with the crowd pouring in to the banquet room. Later she told me Xanax had done the trick.

God willing, Akira will experience a similar level of comfort tonight and tomorrow morning when she exhibits at the art fairs.

Akira's booth is placed adjacent to mine, just as I've requested. From where we sit, the artwork gracing the Temple looks incredible; this does nothing to bolster her self-esteem.

"I only have keychains that anyone can recreate on the internet," she whispers anxiously.

"People will be happy to find a gift option that isn't upwards of forty-something bucks," I assure her. A few potential customers meander by Akira's table, perusing her keychains with interest. Akira's body goes rigid, but she still attempts to squeak out the words to the sales script we've created. Every one of them asks if the Firefox part of the name has to do with the internet browser.

Akira isn't thrilled about standing because she has curvature of the lower spine. A couple of times she fails to grab a paying customer. But all in all, she is doing a fantastic job engaging with the customers.

At the far end of the social hall, she is surprised to see her dad, sister, and sister's boyfriend at the event. She thinks they've come to show emotional support. By the end of the event, she's sold twenty-two of the seventy keychains. "I honestly thought I would only sell five or six," she says, beaming. "It's been a trying endeavor, but I have come out of it with a good chunk of cash."

"How much did you make, Akira?" her dad asks.

"With the tax? About one hundred twenty dollars. A week's paycheck after taxes."

Annie snorts and shakes her head. "I could have made that much money in a snap. I bet people only bought them out of pity, Akira."

Akira's dad puts his arm around her shoulders to comfort her. He knows how hard she's worked to create all those keychains. "You did really well Akira. I'm impressed."

She tells him how scared she'd been to try. "It's all thanks to Jennie's belief that I could do it."

I feel humbled.

While I don't know the sister's side of the story, I can make an educated guess about the source of her resentment.

When there is a child with special needs in the family, parents become obsessed with seeking help for that child. With the spotlight solely shining on that child, the sibling is left out in the dark. There's just so much emotional energy to go around. It's easy for a parent to unintentionally dismisses the sibling's emotional needs.

Engaging in individual and/or family counseling are beneficial techniques of reconnecting with self and other family members. Counseling unearths thornier issues a person may not be willing to face. But it takes trust and willingness to illuminate those negative thoughts and feelings. Sometimes it's just easier to wallow in misery. At least misery is a known factor.

That said, God gives each of us one life to live. We need to wring the heck out of joy and compassion. Misery and jealousy have no place in that equation.

Sunday, there's a craft fair at a synagogue. Akira and I split the price of this booth. There are supposed to be a lot of kids at this event. "Kids like keychains to stick on their backpacks," Akira says.

This time, Akira's dad sits beside her at the table. "I was glad he sat with me so I could know what was going through his mind, judging from his body language," she tells me later.

These kinds of reflective statements still make me wonder about Akira's autism diagnosis.

A few vendors think Akira's keychains are adorable; one vendor even asks if she has considered opening an Etsy shop. In total, ten people walk by her booth. Many of them are kids who run off to ask their parents to buy them a keychain. Their parents think six dollars is too much for a keychain.

Akira does her breathing exercises. "Compared to the other vendors, my keychains are on the lower end of the price range and people still aren't buying them. Still, I'm not giving up hope."

In the end, an older woman and two young girls purchase some keychains. Akira smiles and pockets the money in a small jewelry box her dad bought her during a business trip in Japan.

"Thank you for buying my keychains. Enjoy," she says, waving happily to them.

"How do you feel about how you did this weekend?" I ask.

"Even though I didn't make as much money as I did last night, I still feel accomplished. The total number of keychains I sold? Thirty-three!"

"Once again, you stepped out of your comfort zone and made it happen. Bravo."

Akira just grins.

Anxiety Meltdown

I EXPERIENCE NO TREPIDATION upon receiving Akira's late-night phone call. Flush with pride at her art fair success, she probably is phoning to say, "Thanks again for believing in me."

Then again, I've not taught her how to offer a follow-up message.

"What's up?" I ask warily.

Akira is sobbing into the phone. "My sister pranked me by hiding my new computer gaming charger in the house. I've been frantically searching all over the house. I began rapidly texting my sister at her apartment, begging her to tell me where the cord was."

"How did she respond?"

"She told me I was 'pathetic' for having an anxiety attack. Then she shut off her phone."

I'm incredulous Annie actually stole Akira's new laptop computer. "Did you tell your dad?"

"Dad was watching TV. I was crying so hard, I made snot bubbles and couldn't see. I pleaded with him to do something. He said, 'If you're going to cry, go to your room.'

"My legs went numb. 'I'm having a meltdown and can't move,' I told him.

"Dad didn't seem to care. He just sat there as I bawled."

I attempt to wrap my head around Mark's cool response. "What did he actually say?"

Akira's words rush out in a jumble. "'I'm taking myself out of the equation. I'm done being the bad guy. Duke it out yourselves.'

"How can he expect me to fight my sister and come out unscathed? She is stronger than me, both physically and mentally. It wouldn't be a fair fight."

"How did you react to what he said?"

"After I regained feeling in my legs, I went upstairs to talk to my friends online. Luna and Chloe couldn't believe my sister had done that. It ended up with Luna hunting down my sister on Facebook and ripping into her."

"Call the police and tell them what happened," I advise.

Akira calls me back a minute later. "I'm such a dummy. I should never have called."

"Why? What happened?"

"Once the dispatcher heard I was talking about a charger, she could barely contain her giggles. She said I could report my sister for larceny, but not theft. However, my sister texted to say that since the item is still on the property, it can't be considered theft."

Akira's sobs had camouflaged her words. I'd heard *computer* but not *charger*.

How does Annie even know about the difference between larceny and theft? I wonder.

"You stood up for yourself. That's what's important. Are you going to report her for larceny?"

"I'm too scared."

"Why?"

"Annie will get mad and hurt me."

"Do you really think your sister would hurt you?"

"Yes."

"Do you want to call a mental health hotline? Or you could sleep over at my house."

"I'll come over."

But a few minutes later, she phones back. "I'm going to try talking to Dad again."

"Good. Deep breathing should calm you down. I'll see you for our session tomorrow."

After I click off the phone, I tell Rocky how worried I am about Akira.

"She needs to deal with this, with her own family," he says.

"That seems to be going nowhere fast," I say.

"You're not her mother."

"Yeah, well she could use one right about now," I retort.

"Akira is her father's responsibility, not yours."

"Even if she was a stranger, I'd do all I could to connect her with resources."

"You want to help the world, I know. But too good is no good," he says gently.

"I will never believe that," I say hotly.

Rocky rises from his La-Z-Boy chair. "Get some sleep. You'll see. Akira will be fine tomorrow."

Akira is so panicked from last night's vicious encounter with her sister that she begins puking her guts out during our life-coaching session—this even after taking a Xanax.

"My computer is the one thing that keeps me calm," she says afterward. "You do not take an autistic person's comfort item. This freaks us out worse than anything. My nightly ritual of playing on the computer until midnight was ruined. I wasn't able to sleep all night."

"I'm so sorry you had to go through that. Did you ever get your charger back?"

Akira nods. "Half way through my work shift, I received a text telling me where the power cable was. She had stuck it in a shoebox in the far corner of Dad's closet."

Such childish behavior, especially for someone getting her master's degree in child development, with a thesis on father attachment. "So what precipitated the blowup between you and your sister?"

"About a week ago I received a Christmas gift from one of my managers at work. It contained an assortment of goodies—Lindt truffles, a chocolate Santa, almonds, and a candy cane. I came home from work exhausted and dropped my baggy on the dining room table before going upstairs to take a nap.

"Five p.m. rolled around, and I was awakened by my sister screeching at me to come downstairs. Misty had climbed on the dining room table and ripped apart my gift. She'd eaten three ounces of milk chocolate. I began freaking out because chocolate is lethal to dogs.

"Annie smirked and said Misty needed to be the smart one because I was an idiot. 'This is why you still live at home and will never own your own dog, because you can't even take care of yourself.'"

Akira's sister knows just where to jab the emotional knife.

"By this point, I was crying and showing symptoms of an anxiety attack. Dad called poison control while I bawled like a baby. I'd had no idea Misty was able to get on the dining room table. It didn't help that when we were getting ready to take Misty to the emergency vet, Annie wouldn't hand her to me. I lost what little composure I had and smacked my sister. Snarling angrily, I told her to *go the fuck home.*

"Dad and I drove to the vet and waited several hours before we were allowed to take Misty home. During that time, my sister took it upon herself to punish me for smacking her. She went into my room and hid the power cable to my computer."

So that explains her sister's over-the-top reaction.

Akira makes another dash for the toilet.

I am not perturbed. My gut says the vomiting is a positive sign of flushing all the emotional garbage out of her system.

"Sorry to make such a fool of myself," she says, wiping her lips with the back of her hand.

"On the contrary. All these years, you believed your parents and sister were the only people who knew the true Akira. But in the last eighteen months, you've glimpsed your authentic self, reflected in the eyes of your fellow Toastmasters, store manager, colleagues, job coach, congregants, and me."

"I guess?"

I put my hands on my hips. "Is that a question or a statement?"

She smiles wanly. "A statement." She requires a constant reminder to voice her feelings as statements rather than questions.

After she cleans herself up and guzzles some ginger ale to settle her stomach, we discuss calling a few mental health professionals, despite it being the Thursday before Christmas. Akira's new therapist is out of town, and she has no one taking her calls. Akira says she first needs to phone the Autism Society. "I want to ask about ways to get me out of the house and away from my demon of a sister."

Surprisingly, Sheri, her advocate at the autism organization, answers the phone. She gives Akira a few numbers to call and tells her to "hang in there."

It turns out the hotline and subsidized housing sites are also closed for the holidays. How strange. The holidays are often the time of year when all hell breaks loose.

"What am I going to do?" Akira laments. "I feel unsafe at home. My sister can pick my bedroom lock, walk into my room at any time, and take whatever she wants."

"Has Annie ever taken anything else of yours besides the charger?" I ask.

"Last month she wanted to play one of my new anime games. I told her 'no,' so she came over to the house while I was at work and took the game."

"What did your dad say?"

"Nothing. Annie finally brought it back."

"How about installing a new lock on your bedroom door?"

"Annie will pick that lock, too, and Dad doesn't want to ruin the woodwork around my door by installing a chain lock or bolt."

"How about installing a new bolt lock on the front door?"

Akira wrings her hands. "Dad says Annie is his daughter, and this is her house, too."

She dashes to the bathroom again. In her absence, I phone the rabbi and relay the whole story. I've only lived in North Carolina for twenty months, but he grew up here and knows everybody in town. "Do you know of a congregational family who would rent her a room in their house, or do you have other suggestions?"

After a brief silence, the rabbi says, "I'm sorry to say, this is beyond my resources. She should contact the Jewish Federation after the holidays are over. What else would you like me to do?"

I answer without a moment's hesitation. "Can you call Akira's dad and ask him to get a lock for her door?"

"That I can do," says the rabbi. "I don't know how successful I will be, though."

Akira returns from the bathroom. Her face is splotchy from sobbing.

"I just phoned the rabbi. He's calling your dad."

Akira shivers. "Dad's going to be furious with me. He'll take away my privileges to use the computer."

"First of all, you're not a teenager, where he has the authority to take away your privileges. Secondly, you paid for your new computer, not him. You have control over when and when not to use it."

Akira dabs at her eyes. "Dad will be mad about the rabbi knowing our business, too. He always says that what happens in our house stays in our house. We don't want to look bad in the community."

"People threaten to harm their spouse or child if they report their physical or sexual abuse and neglect. These victims lead lives of quiet desperation. But your dad isn't going to physically hurt you."

"I know, but I'm also petrified that Annie will find out and verbally abuse me to the point that I will do something worse than smacking her."

This discussion is too intense for me to handle alone. I know of only one other social worker to call. I peck Tracey's number into my phone. She is a friend who moved here from Chicago.

Tracey and I went out to dinner a few nights ago, and I told her what was going on with Akira. I didn't worry about a privacy issue because Akira is fine with us writing/publishing her travails.

But I'd forgotten that today Tracey is packing to go visit her daughter in California. When she answers the phone, she is unusually curt for yet another reason; I neglected to notify her beforehand that Akira would be calling her. Foul ball for this ADHD batter.

I sit across the card table from Akira as she puts Tracey on loudspeaker and shares her story. Tracey agrees a lock on the door is absolutely necessary.

"Do you feel like you want to hurt yourself?" Tracey asks her.

"Not at this point, but if my sister's verbal abuse keeps up, I'm afraid I'll do something I'll regret."

"And what would that be?"

"I don't know. I'm scared to go home. Dad isn't doing diddly squat to make me feel safe."

I interrupt to explain that earlier we had gone to Home Depot to look for door locks for Akira's bedroom. All the options would have required her to drill screws into the doorframe.

"I'm terrified that Dad won't let me modify my own doors," cries Akira. "He'll say I'm being childish and I need to suck it up."

"I suggest you go to hospital emergency and admit yourself for an evaluation," says Tracey. "At least you will be out of your house and in a safe place over the holiday weekend. Then you can see your therapist next week."

"My dad will get mad and reprimand me if I do that."

"Right now, you are fighting for your own survival," says Tracey. "Don't worry about your dad's feelings, do what is right for you."

Just as we prepare to leave for the hospital, Akira receives a text from her dad saying, "Stay where you are. I'm coming to get you." She blanches. "Dad only sends a text like this when it's urgent or he's really upset."

Minutes later, my doorbell rings.

Akira sobs into her hands. "What do I do? I'm scared. I don't feel safe at home."

"You don't have to go anywhere you don't want, kiddo," I assure her.

"But he's going to make me. When he gets angry like this, he won't listen to reason."

Mark walks into the hallway and looms over her. Akira looks frantic.

"Pack up your things. You're coming home," he says calmly.

Akira edges into a leather chair. "No. I don't feel safe at home."

"I have no clue what she's talking about," he says.

"She can't have Annie busting into her room whenever she wants," I reply.

"She's overreacting," says Mark. "Get your stuff, Akira. You'll be fine once you go back to your room with all your stuffed animals, the dog, and your computer—all the things you love."

"I'm not going home, Dad," says Akira, sniffling.

"Akira, you're making a fool of your family, calling the rabbi, the Jewish Federation, the whole world."

"That's how desperate she feels, Mark," I say. "You don't want her to attempt suicide, do you?"

He dismisses my assertion. "She's not going to try to commit suicide. She never has before."

"Actually, I tried when I was in middle school," admits Akira.

"When?" Mark's tone is sharp.

"One time I got in a fight with Annie and I ran out of the house and sat on the university steps till a cop told me to go home. None of you came after me, so when I got home, I took a big knife from the kitchen drawer and brought it to my room. You guys never came in to check on me and I was really feeling like killing myself, but I didn't."

"I never knew anything about a knife, but I know you're not going to kill yourself now."

"Then you need to make her feel safe," I say. "Would you consider putting a chain or bolt lock on her bedroom door?"

He hesitates as he stares at his daughter. "It's definitely something we could talk about."

I turn to Akira. "Will you feel comfortable going home if your dad puts a lock on your door?"

Tears slosh down Akira's cheeks. "It's only a temporary solution. I need to get out of there."

"Then where do you want to go?" Mark asks, exasperated.

"I talked to a social worker friend of Jennie's, and she suggests I get evaluated at the hospital."

Mark's body stiffens. "That's ridiculous. You already know what the evaluation will say. They'll put you in a home with strangers. Would that be better than living with me? We'll have to go through all sorts of legal proceedings to get you back. Is that what you want?"

Akira stoops over in her chair, sobbing. "I don't know. I don't know."

I sense a dose of tough-love is needed here. "Akira, you are twenty-eight years old. Nobody can make you do anything you don't want to do. Do you want to sleep at my house tonight, go for the hospital evaluation, or go home?"

"I don't know," she sobs.

"If you don't know, we don't know," I say. "Nobody can make that decision but you."

Akira looks at her dad and me as she dries her eyes. "I think the best thing for me to do is get the evaluation. I am going to the hospital. I'm scared of what I might do to myself if I don't."

"Get in the car. I'll take you," says Mark.

Fat chance of that happening. I toss Akira my car keys. "Get into my car. I'll drive. Dad can follow us."

Akira's dad sighs and gets into his car.

On our drive to the hospital, I tell Akira she is my hero. "I would have just given in and gone home. But even at your darkest moment, you still had the strength to do what was right for you."

"Took me long enough," she snickers. "I'm really upset I allowed myself to get so sick."

"You puked out all the dishonesty and disrespect you've been feeling."

Akira's body relaxes. "I didn't see it that way before. I really wanted to make Dad happy, but I just couldn't do it. I just don't feel safe there."

At that moment, Tracey calls back. Akira and I update her.

I speak into the Bluetooth. "Isn't she brave?"

"You really are, Akira," says Tracey. "By the way, you're not a minor, so those were lies your dad told you about being sent to live with strangers and having to go through legal proceedings to get you back."

Akira breathes a sigh of relief.

"You made a good decision about going in for the evaluation," says Tracey. "You'll be watched 24/7 for a couple of days. You'll have time to decide what you want to do. Jennie will drop you off at the emergency entrance. Then you can go to the front desk and ask to be admitted."

Minutes later, we drive past Mark as he searches for a parking space in the hospital lot.

"Let me out," says Akira. "I want to go in myself, without Dad trying to talk me out of it."

"Okay, Akira, go for it," I say. "Good luck."

Akira jumps out of my car, clutching her laptop like a lifeline, and rushes through the emergency room doors.

I proceed to the main hospital entrance to pick up my husband after his outpatient procedure. I'm dashing down the hospital corridor when my cell phone rings. It's Mark.

"Hey," he says. "On the drive over, I did a lot of thinking. I guess I didn't realize how serious this thing was with Akira. I'm just tired of always being the bad guy between my girls."

"I'm so glad you came to that conclusion. Now you can begin a new relationship with Akira and be her hero. She just wants you to stand up for her."

"I figured they could fight it out between themselves."

"It would never be a fair fight between someone with autism and someone who's a bully."

"Maybe you're right," he agrees.

"You going to get that lock for her door?" I ask.

"I'll look into it."

I click off the phone, overcome with euphoria. Time and time again, God enables me to make a difference in this girl/woman's life. I am blessed.

A couple of hours later, Akira phones. "How did it go?" I ask.

"They admitted me to the psychiatric ward. A nurse asked me a few questions before taking a few vials of blood to test. They wanted to make sure I hadn't attempted to overdose before getting there. My laptop, clothes, and cellphone were bagged, and I was dressed in a pair of maroon-colored paper scrubs and those weird navy socks with rubber gripping the soles.

"Normally I'm scared of needles, but for some bizarre reason, I actually welcomed the pain from this one. That realization frightened me. A few hours later I was given an evaluation.

"They asked me if I was feeling suicidal and if there was anything in my house that could be considered a suicide device.

"I told them practically everything in my room could be used in that way. I have this magic wand in my room. If I bashed it against my head enough, I could go unconscious.

"They asked if my family has any guns. I told them about a BB gun somewhere in storage.

"Then they asked if I would use it, and I told them I don't know. I've only fired nerf and water guns before.

"I answered a few more questions about my age, ethnicity, my living situation, and a few other personal questions. They deemed it necessary for me to stay the night for surveillance."

Listening to Akira's recital, my eyes are teary. "You rescued yourself tonight."

"I guess?"

"Question or statement?" I tease.

"Statement," she says.

Aftermath

THE NEXT DAY, I received a phone call from Akira. "I guess I wasn't suicidal after all. The hospital discharged me and said the hospital social worker would help me find subsidized housing. In the meantime, they agree I am not safe at home. They told Dad to change the lock on my bedroom door until I can find a new place to live."

"Excellent. How is your dad taking the news?"

"Surprisingly well. In fact, we've been looking at apartments. I think we found something. It's pet-friendly, one-bedroom, in a safe community, and close to work. "

This apartment search is a surprise to me. "How are you going to afford to pay your rent on the part-time salary you make at the pet store?"

"Dad is going to co-sign with me and pay the rent," Akira says, excitedly.

Evidently he prefers paying rent over drilling a hole into her bedroom door frame. "That is so awesome. Will your dad give your sister your address?"

"Nope," says Akira. "We're going to hide the paperwork."

"Because otherwise there is zero use in you moving," I add.

"No, I know that."

"So you'll finally feel safe?"

"Yeah."

"Tell me about the apartment complex."

"It's got a pool, a place to walk Misty, and a laundry room directly across from my building. But I might still bring my laundry home to do."

My voice gets snarky. "You do your own laundry at home. You can certainly do your own laundry at the apartment site."

"Dad's worried I won't keep the new place clean."

"That's not his concern. You can keep your apartment as neat or messy as you want. We'll go over the basics together, once you move."

"What basics?"

"You need to wipe down the stove and kitchen table after you eat, vacuum and wash the floors once a week, throw your dirty clothes in the hamper, and hang up your clean clothes as soon as you come home from work. Also, remove your shoes and tell visitors to do the same when they walk into your apartment. This will keep germs and dirt out of the house."

"That's a lot."

"You'll be fine," I assure her.

"I gotta go. We're going back for a second look today."

"Okay. Good luck and enjoy. Before you go, let me talk to your dad."

Mark's tenor voice comes on the line.

"Hey, Mark," I say. "I just want to tell you how proud I am of you for being so emotionally supportive of Akira. It's awesome you're paying her rent. Just be positive with her. Tell her you know she can do this."

I hear the smile in his voice. "It's been good."

As I click off the phone, I wonder what factor finally drove Akira's dad to take action. Was it embarrassment over the rabbi's phone call, the Jewish Federation's knowledge of what was going on, or Akira's hospital admittance that illuminated the moment of truth? Whatever the catalyst, it's a new beginning for Akira.

That night, as I slip into bed, warm and cozy beneath my down comforter, I ponder how from sky view each of us appears as a speck of sand. But despite our apparent insignificance, God breathes hope and compassion into our souls in order to change the world. Each of us possess the ability to think and dream. It's our parents' or guardians' jobs to encourage and assist us to self-actualize without fear, to act as God's partners in repairing the world. To fully engage in this life, rather than merely view it as a weigh station leading to whatever—if any—afterlife follows.

All of us, at some point in our lives, experience physical, mental, or emotional challenges. For some, these challenges are lifelong. As we each face our own challenges, I pray that God reaches into our sorrows and grants us the spark of hope. Just as we each need someone to believe in us, we need to mentor those in need, be it family, friend, or the homeless guy on the corner. By helping each other attain our goals, we will grow as human beings and as a society.

Final Reckoning

A FEW DAYS LATER, Akira and I meet for our weekly session. "How's it going?"

"Evidently, my hospital stay was enough to show Dad that the situation was more dire than he'd thought," says Akira. "He apologized to me and suggested we start looking for another apartment for me."

"I thought you guys already found a place."

"Actually, that one was a bit too far from work. We found another apartment that was a good price, very close to work, pet friendly, and in a safe complex."

"And how have you been feeling emotionally?"

"I haven't had a massive anxiety attack since Dad stepped up to the plate. Now I have my friends, you, and Dad on my side. Independent living, here I come!"

I hug Akira. "I am so proud of you."

Akira bows her head. "By the way, Dad wants me to cut our sessions to two hours, instead of two-and-a-half, per week."

I experience a surge of anger. "Akira, you've got to stop giving over your control to your father. You can certainly afford to pay an additional thirty dollars a week from the money in your savings account."

"It's not him," she blurts out. "It's me."

I feel blindsided. "*You* want to cut back to two hours a week?"

She nods. "I want to save up to pay for my utilities and food."

"So it is a money thing, after all?"

"I just think I'm ready," she says quietly.

Joy douses my anger. "Really?"

"I didn't want to hurt your feelings, so that's why I said it was Dad's idea."

This is the goal every teacher, tutor, or life coach hopes for—the ability of their student to stand on her or his own two feet. I predict we'll totally be finished working together in the next six months.

"I was waiting for you to reach this point," I say. "Mazel Tov for being able to tell me what you need. If this is your decision, I'm all for it."

Akira grins

"After life coaching you, I think I want to do this from now on," I say.

Akira does a double take. "Are you saying I was your first life coaching client?"

I grin. "Guess some abilities just come naturally!"

About the Author

Jennie Spallone possesses a master's degree in special education as well as advanced certification in higher-level thinking skills. The former special education teacher authored two written expression and grammar texts and has delivered presentations on these multisensory programs at teacher conferences throughout the Midwest.

Besides teaching grades 1 through 12, Jennie mentored college seniors majoring in special education. She also developed and presented professional growth and development courses for general education teachers.

For nearly two decades, Jennie has operated a successful tutoring practice, specializing in dyslexia, ADD, and Asperger's. She also works as a part-time college academic coach.

The author is known for her suspense novels. *Smashing Castles* is her first narrative non-fiction.

Book Discussion Questions

1. What was your initial impression of Akira? How, if at all, did your opinion change?

2. How would you describe Akira's relationship with her sister?

3. How was Mark's relationship different with each of his daughters?

4. How did Akira's autism diagnosis affect her family's attitude and actions toward her, first as a child, then as a young adult?

5. What role did Damon serve for Akira, even though he lived thousands of miles away? Why does she feel so comfortable with him?

6. Why did Akira feel like she was a visitor in her own house?

7. What were the underlying causes of Annie's acting-out behavior with her sister?

8. When Mark was together with both daughters, did the level of verbal abuse going on between the two girls change? If yes, why?

9. How did Akira hope her surgery would impact the family?

10. Reflecting upon Mark's response/lack of response in creating a respectful environment for the family to interact, what would you have done differently?

11. Why did Akira endure such verbal abuse? What happened when her core belief was disputed by her dad?

12. How did the life coach play a meaningful role in Akira's life?

13. What are the life coach's core beliefs about raising and teaching children? Tell why you agree/disagree with her thesis.

14. What was the driving force that finally convinced Mark to find an apartment for Akira? Why do you think he waited so long before acting?

15. By the end of the book, how do the following people change, if at all: Akira, Annie, Mark, life coach?

Autism Resources

I have not personally reviewed these websites, but they could be useful as you search for additional information about autism.

Parents/Guardians

- Top 10 Autism Websites Recommended by Parents (Eden II Programs)

  https://eden2.org/top-10-autism-websites-recommended-by-parents/

  Autism Speaks provides a comprehensive resource guide for all states. The site also boasts an impressive list of apps that parents may find useful.

Mental Health

- What Is Autism Spectrum Disorder? (American Psychiatric Association)

  https://www.psychiatry.org/patients-families/autism/what-is-autism-spectrum-disorder

  The American Academy of Pediatrics recommends that children be screened. Many national and local advocacy organizations provide information and resources.

Pediatricians/Hospitals

- Autism Initiatives (AAP.org)

  https://www.aap.org/en-us/advocacy-and-policy/aap-health-initiatives/Pages/autism-initiatives.aspx

  You will find information about autism tools and resources for pediatricians. Also provides early language and social milestones in a checklist format.

- Which Doctors Treat Autism Spectrum Disorders? (US News & World Report)

  https://health.usnews.com/health-care/patient-advice/articles/2018-03-16/which-doctors-treat-autism-spectrum-disorders

  Mar 16, 2018 — The National Institutes of Health reports that ASD now stands as the umbrella for autism disorders. Visit the resources page to determine whether there is a nutritional trigger for some types of ASD.

- Autism Resources (Mark Bertin, M.D., Developmental Pediatrics)

  https://www.developmentaldoctor.com/autism/

  Provides a list of recommended reading material, articles, and other resources.

- Center for Autism Spectrum Disorders (Nationwide Children's Hospital)

  https://www.nationwidechildrens.org/specialties/center-for-autism-spectrum-disorders

  Serving the needs of children with an Autism Spectrum Disorder and their quality of life. Learn more about ASD and services.

Professionals

- National Professional Development Center on Autism Spectrum Disorder

  https://autismpdc.fpg.unc.edu/national-professional-development-center-autism-spectrum-disorder

  Since 2007, the National Professional Development Center on Autism Spectrum Disorder (NPDC) has worked to develop free professional resources, including modules that demonstrate evidence-based practices.

- 40 Autism Teaching Resources You Should Know About (Special Needs Resource Blog)

  https://specialneedsresourceblog.com/2016/04/22/40-autism-teaching-resources-you-should-know-about/

  Provides a list of teacher blogs, classroom management tips, and lesson plans for teaching autistic students.

Schools

- Recognized Schools for Children with Autism (TheBestSchools.org)

  https://thebestschools.org/features/recognized-schools-for-children-with-autism/

  List includes nationally recognized schools, as well as schools which have ... professionals, neurologists, and pediatricians within the community and also host monthly meetings and speaking events.

CPSIA information can be obtained
at www.ICGtesting.com
Printed in the USA
FFHW011831030919
54639533-60332FF